STRANDED ON THE
INFORMATION HIGHWAY

STRANDED ON THE INFORMATION HIGHWAY

By
John Levesque

Mosaic Press
Oakville, ON. - Buffalo, N.Y.

Canadian Cataloguing in Publication Data

Levesque, John, 1953-
    Stranded on the information highway

ISBN   0-88962-608-1

1.   Information superighway - Humor.   2.   Canadian wit and humor (English.* I. Title.

PS8573.E96183S73   1996   C818'.5402   C96-930830-2
PR9199.3.L48S73   1996

Published by MOSAIC PRESS, P.O. Box 1032, Oakville, Ontario, L6J 5E9, Canada. Offices and warehouse at 1252 Speers Road, Units #1&2, Oakville, Ontario, L6L 5N9, Canada and Mosaic Press, 85 River Rock Drive, Suite 202, Buffalo, N.Y., 14207, USA.

Mosaic Press acknowledges the assistance of the Canada Council, the Ontario Arts Council and the Dept. of Canadian Heritage, Government of Canada, for their support of our publishing programme.

Text layout by Sanchia Greenwood
Cover and book design by Susan Parker
Printed and bound in Canada
ISBN   0-88962-608-1

In Canada:
MOSAIC PRESS, 1252 Speers Road, Units #1&2, Oakville, Ontario, L6L 5N9, Canada. P.O. Box 1032, Oakville, Ontario, L6J 5E9
In the United States:
MOSAIC PRESS, 85 River Rock Drive, Suite 202, Buffalo, N.Y., 14207
In the UK and Western Europe:
DRAKE INTERNATIONAL SERVICES, Market House, Market Place, Deddington, Oxford. OX15 OSF

For my mother

Where is the wisdom we have lost in knowledge?
Where is the knowledge we have lost in information?
—T.S. Eliot

TABLE OF CONTENTS

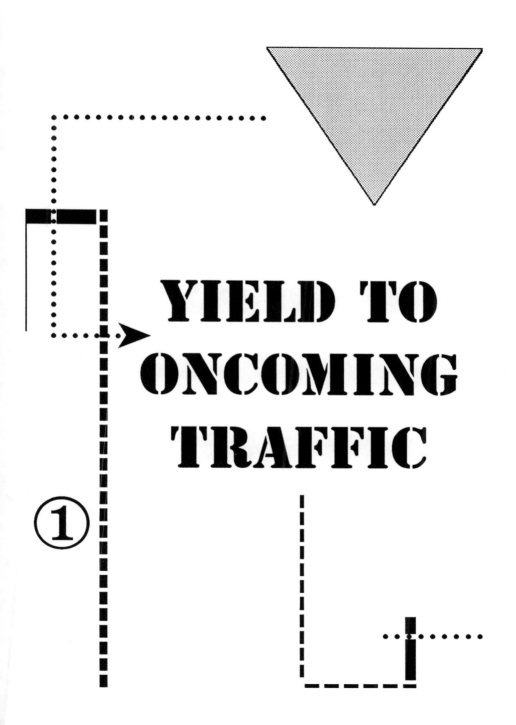

YIELD TO ONCOMING TRAFFIC

①

BRAND LOYALTY

Jim sauntered into the corner store and asked for a large king-size pack of Smoking Can Kill You.

"Say again?" said Dan, the proprietor of the store, who didn't recognize Jim as one of his regular customers.

"Smoking Can Kill You," Jim said. "Large king-size."

"I never heard of that brand," Dan said as he scanned his shelves of cigarettes. "The closest we have is Cigarettes Cause Fatal Lung Disease. Is Smoking Can Kill You a new brand?"

"No," Jim said. "I've been buying them for the past few weeks, but I'm new in town. They have a nice smooth flavour is what I like about them."

"I'll have to ask my distributor about them," Dan said.

Larry, who was one of Dan's regular customers, entered the store. "Hey Larry," said Dan, "have you ever heard of a brand of cigarettes called Smoking Can Kill You?"

"Nope," Larry said as he approached the counter, "but they're always coming out with new brands." He looked at Jim. "Is that what you smoke?"

Jim nodded. "They're not menthol or anything but they have a coolness, you know."

Larry nodded and said, "Maybe you could try Tobacco Causes Fatal Lung Disease In Non-Smokers. It's a smooth enough smoke, though I try to cut back a bit when I've got company over."

Dan ran his finger along a shelf of cigarettes until he found a pack of Tobacco Causes Fatal Lung Disease In Non-Smokers. The brand name was boldly displayed in white letters on a black background. In smaller letters near the bottom corner of the pack was the word Player's. Dan wasn't sure what that word meant.

"I used to buy Smoking During Pregnancy Can Harm Your Baby," Jim said, "but after a while I thought it was too much of a woman's cigarette, if you know what I mean. No bite to it or anything."

Larry nodded. "My wife smokes Smoking During Pregnancy Can Harm Your Baby. She tried switching to Cigarettes Cause Cancer but they bothered her throat."

Fred, who rented the small apartment above the store, came in the door. "Hey Dan, could you give me a carton of Tobacco Smoke Can Harm Your Children?"

"I can't give it to you," Dan said with a sly glance at Larry, "but I can sell it to you."

"Fair enough," said Fred. "How's it going, Larry?"

"I've still got that damn cough," Larry said. "Hey, Fred, have you ever heard of a brand of cigarettes called Smoking Can Kill You?"

"Yep," Fred said. "My brother-in-law smokes them. He says he likes the name. Direct, you know."

Dan nodded toward Jim. "This fellow here is new in town and he was looking for them. My distributor doesn't seem to handle them or something."

"Sure he does," Fred said. "Just ask for them by name next time you see him. Apparently it's the fastest growing brand of cigarettes on the market right now."

"Is that so," said Dan.

"Where does your brother-in-law get them?" Jim asked Fred.

"At the drug mart," Fred said.

Jim nodded.

Dan looked over his shoulder at the cigarette shelves and said, "It's funny the way people attach themselves to a particular brand of smokes. Personally, I couldn't tell the difference between Cigarettes Cause Strokes And Heart Disease and Cigarettes Cause Cancer if I was paid to. I guess folks just go for the sound of certain brand names, like with their favourite beer."

Fred nodded. "Can I have that carton now, Dan?"

"Oh, sorry, Fred," Dan said. He handed Fred a carton of Tobacco Smoke Can Harm Your Children and Fred handed him two twenties.

"The cigarette companies do a lot of market testing before they introduce a new brand," Larry said. "They sit down with what's called a focus group and they bounce a few brand names off them. I heard that a bad reaction from a focus group actually killed one new brand."

"What brand was that?" Dan asked him as he fished in the cash register for change.

"It was called Smoking Is Not A Good Idea. The focus group thought the name was too wishy-washy."

"They were right," said Fred as he took his change from Dan. "I've got to run, guys. See you later."

"I don't know," Dan said, "I kind of like that approach. Smoking Is Not A Good Idea. . . I think I'd try a cigarette by that name."

"But you haven't tried Smoking Can Kill You," Jim said.

"No I haven't," Dan agreed.

"Don't knock it 'til you've tried it. How far's the nearest drug mart from here?"

"About six blocks," Dan said.

"Guess I'll grab a cab," Jim said as he pushed the door open. "Do you want me to bring you a pack or two to try?"

"For me?" Dan said. "No way. Cigarettes Are Addictive."

"Okay," Jim said with a shrug. "You want a carton of those?"

"Sure," Dan said. "That'll hold me until the distributor comes on Monday."

THE TOILET OF BABEL

Waves of immigration and rapid advances in technology have contributed to the development of a true global village in which everyone can communicate with everyone else, but no one necessarily understands what anyone else is saying. An item of information as seemingly trivial as the label on the door of a public washroom can become an overwhelming obstacle for someone who doesn't grasp the language or customs of the people who devised the label. For example, on my first visit to Great Britain a number of years ago, I was perplexed by the letters WC visible on certain doors in hotels, restaurants, train stations and airports. I wondered what these two letters could possibly stand for: Waiting Chamber? Wing Commander? Wart Cauterizer?

My wife, who had more experience in the British way of life, informed me that WC stood for "water closet".

"And what does 'water closet' stand for?" I asked her.

"Washroom," she said.

"Then why don't they just call it that?"

"They do, sometimes — except they refer to it as the loo."

My line of argument that day was not without merit. But it overlooked the fact that "washroom" was also a euphemism, since most of us go to the washroom not to wash but to go the bathroom. Of course, "go to the bathroom" is also a euphemism. In fact, the multitude of words we use to describe the place where we relieve ourselves (yet another euphemism) is the semantic equivalent of one of those Russian dolls that contain a maddening number of smaller and identical dolls inside. By the time we've finally reached the smallest doll, chances are we've wet our pants.

If I, who understood and spoke English, had trouble deciphering something as basic as the official British euphemism for a washroom, how could someone from a more faraway country and culture possibly overcome this information gap in time? That question was undoubtedly on the minds of the engineers who decided it would be better to use a symbol rather than the letters WC or the word "loo" to label the door that leads to a personal hygiene station (still another euphemism).

The people whose task was to come up with a symbol probably reckoned a pictorial emblem of a toilet would do the job. But then it occurred to them that there is no standardized universal toilet in the global village. Some toilets are flushed by hand, some are flushed by a foot pedal, some are flushed by yanking a chain from above, and some are holes in the ground with no flush mechanism whatsoever. Which of these toilets could accurately serve as a symbol on the universal washroom door?

The compromise solution, conceived some years ago, was to sidestep the problem of a viable toilet emblem by attaching a depiction of respective human figures, denoting the male and female gender, to washroom doors. The rationale behind these symbols was that people were bright enough to deduce for themselves where the doors led.

This non-verbal approach to the problem seemed to make perfect sense in the polyglot, multicultural world of the late twentieth century. Nowadays, symbols of all kinds serve a purpose once served by words. Our roadways abound in emblems that inform, instruct or admonish us, depending on the circumstances. No aspect of our lives is untouched by abstract renderings of words or ideas. From the symbol of the leaping deer on the side of the highway to the small light atop confessional booths in Catholic churches, we are constantly called upon to interpret symbols and to act in accordance with them.

Unfortunately, symbols can sometimes be as perplexing as the words they were designed to replace. A case in point was the day my wife and I were hurtling along the highway when, on the dashboard of our Japanese-designed car, a small circle with an exclamation mark inside it suddenly flashed a brilliant red. I asked my wife if she knew what a circle with an exclamation mark meant. She said she didn't. The only thing we could agree on was that an exclamation mark usually appeared at the end of a sentence in which an emphatic point was being made. Unfortunately, we had no idea what point our automobile was trying to make. I had visions of being engulfed in a fireball before we found the appropriate translation of the exclamation mark in the owner's manual. Someone more versed in automotive lore later explained that an exclamation mark within a circle signified brake trouble.

Even the simple gender symbols that adorn the doors of most public washrooms can lead to problems of interpretation. The symbols on the doors in our part of the world depict a stick-figure female in a dress or skirt and a stick-figure man in trousers. For some reason, perhaps owing to slight brain damage, I have trouble immediately distinguishing one stick figure from another. I usually have to linger for an embarrassing second look to ensure that the trousers are indeed trousers and the skirt is indeed a skirt.

If I have trouble sorting out these washroom symbols, imagine the problems they could cause persons from places in the world where the skirt/trouser dividing line is not culturally imprinted. How would a male Scottish Highlander or a Maori from New Zealand, both of whom have been known to wear skirts, decide which washroom to use? And how could an individual from the remote rain forests of Papua New Guinea, who wears a loincloth at best, possibly know how to operate the toilet if and when he managed to select the right door?

These questions may seem trivial at first glance, but most catastrophes have a way of starting out small.

REACH OUT AND HOLD

In medieval times, people who owned and operated castles and fortresses kept their premises safe from intruders in a variety of ingenious ways. They erected thick stone walls that could withstand slings, arrows and sometimes even battering rams. Then they dug a moat around the building and stocked the moat with flesh-eating creatures from exotic lands. Then they designed a bridge across the moat that could be drawn up at the medieval equivalent of a moment's notice. If intruders were still intent on besieging the castle or fortress, the owners of the building also deployed spear-carriers to stand guard in the turrets, from where they could fling their weapons down upon the intruders. When it was available, boiling oil was sometimes poured on would-be marauders as a kind of medieval practical joke whose punchline was entirely lost on the people on the receiving end of the oil.

If none of these tactics prevented the marauders from overrunning the fortress, the general feeling was that the marauders deserved to overrun it. So the fortress changed hands and the marauders were now in charge of the stone walls, the moat, the flesh-eating creatures, the drawbridge, the spear-carriers and the boiling oil.

From our relatively lofty vantage point here in the present, these medieval notions of security and defence seem laughably crude. Contemporary fortresses and castles, which mainly house CEOs and their corporate armies, are protected by "clean", sophisticated devices such as motion-detecting alarm systems, electronic pass-card slots and networks of video cameras and monitors. But the single most effective weapon in the current security arsenal − a weapon that prevents virtually any unwanted human being from breaching the corporate perimeter − is its electronic telephone-answering system.

For corporations, the beauty of automated telephone answering is twofold:

1. It reduces the necessity to employ excessive numbers of human beings, who can become a major hindrance to shareholder dividends.

2. When it's operating at peak capacity, the new system can effectively fend off any and all calls.

The new telephone-answering technology accomplishes this not by threatening bodily harm to people who try to place incoming calls, but by wearing them down psychologically until they have lost all interest in speaking to anyone within the building. The system is diabolically subtle. When a person places a phone call to a company or institution, a soothing recorded voice usually female comes on the line and informs the caller why he or she should give up all hope of ever speaking to an actual human being.

Here's a brief sample of what an incoming caller might hear:

"Welcome to Telcomp Services Incorporated. If you are presently holding your telephone in your right hand, please transfer it to your left hand to facilitate the button-pressing you will momentarily be called upon to perform. If you are holding a dial telephone, please hang up and never call us again.

"If you know the name and voice-mail extension of the person to whom you wish to speak, please check beforehand with our automated human resources data base to ensure that this person is still employed by this company and holds the same voice-mail extension. Our auto-mated human resources data base can be accessed through the follow-ing toll-free number. . .

"In the unlikely event you are still on the line, please indicate by pressing the appropriate button whether you wish to communicate with this system in English, French, or any of the sixteen other languages now serviced by this system. Please choose now. . .

"Our Swahili answering service will come on-line in a moment. Please hold. If you have made an error in selecting the language in which you would like to be served and you now wish to countermand that order, please hang up and use the following toll-free number to liaise with our patented Fail-Safe Command Override Centre. . .

"In the unlikely event you are still on the line, please hold until one of our input vectors is free. In the likely event that the person you wish to speak to is away from his or her desk and you instead liaise with that person's electronic voice-mail, please keep your message brief and intelligible. . .

"One of our input vectors is now free. If the astrological sign of the person with whom you wish to speak is Capricorn, Aquarius or Pisces, please press 1. If Neptune is retrograde in this person's solar eighth house, please press 2. If Saturn is transiting this person's tenth house, please press. . ."

ON THE ROAD TO RECOVERY

A pair of enterprising New York City psychologists have launched a mobile therapy service in which patients who are pressed for time can bare their soul while being chauffeured to and from work, appointments, the airport or nowhere special. The business is called Mobile Psychological Services. It operates out of a well-equipped, soundproof van with tinted windows. So far, forty people have signed on for this unique form of therapy. The following is a rare glimpse into one such session.

PATIENT *(after blowing his nose with a tissue taken from a box on a small table between two plush chairs on which he and the doctor are seated):* I don't know what it is, I just feel that my life is spinning out of control.

DOCTOR *(to the driver of the van via intercom):* We're hemmed in here, Roger. Make a left turn the first chance you get. *(To the patient.)* How do you mean, out of control?

PATIENT: Well, I guess I —

DOCTOR *(to the driver via intercom):* Forget what I just said. Instead of turning left, swing into the right lane and try that bypass idea through the Village we were discussing yesterday. *(To the patient.)* Sorry. Go ahead.

PATIENT: It doesn't seem there's any part of the day that I have control over anymore. I feel as if I'm being pulled in so many different—

DOCTOR: Excuse me a second. *(To the driver.)* Nix the bypass idea, Roger. The Holland Tunnel's a nightmare at this time of day with all the upstate commuters. Try hanging a left. *(To the patient.)* I'm so sorry. You said you were being pulled or something?

PATIENT: I feel I can't handle the pace of my life anymore. From the moment I wake up, it's as if my whole day is pre-programmed. There's not one spare or spontaneous moment in it.

DOCTOR: I see.

PATIENT: If there were just some way of reclaiming a small fraction of my life, maybe I could — *(The intercom buzzes.)*

DOCTOR: Excuse me. *(To the driver.)* What is it, Roger?

DRIVER: Our next patient is at the Midtown Skyport. If I turn left now, we'll never get there in time.

DOCTOR *(irritably):* So figure out your own route. I'm trying to work here. *(To the patient.)* I apologize for the interruption. Tell me a bit more about this idea of reclaiming your life.

PATIENT *(haltingly):* What I would do is take Twelfth Street to Second Avenue, then Twenty-Third Street to Roosevelt Avenue. That would get you to the Skyport in plenty of time.

DOCTOR: That's an idea. Could I ask you to repeat that to the driver on this intercom?

PATIENT *(takes the intercom from the doctor):* You could try turning right on Twelfth Street, then left on Second Avenue, then right on Twenty-Third Street all the way to Roosevelt.

DRIVER: No can do. They're shooting a movie in Gramercy Park this week. The whole area's cordoned off.

PATIENT: I see. *(To the doctor.)* I should have known that.

DOCTOR: Nonsense. How could you possibly have known?

DRIVER: Maybe I could take Twentieth instead of Twenty-Third.

DOCTOR *(to the patient):* What do you think?

PATIENT: It might work.

DOCTOR *(to the driver):* Okay. Try Twentieth instead of Twenty-Third. But you've got to avoid Washington Square, and remember they're still resurfacing Bleecker Street.

DRIVER: I'm changing course right now.

DOCTOR *(to the driver):* Roger.

DRIVER: Yes?

DOCTOR *(to the driver):* Nothing. I meant 'Roger', as in 'ten-four.'

DRIVER: I don't know walkie-talkie lingo.

DOCTOR *(To the patient):* I'm so sorry about all these interruptions. You said you felt as if your whole day was pre-programmed?

PATIENT: There was a time when I was on top of everything, when nothing was too much for me: my work life, my family life, our social schedule. But now, every day when I wake up, I feel a tightness right here in my—

DOCTOR: You know, something just occurred to me.

PATIENT *(expectantly):* Yes?

DOCTOR: I think I may have figured out the problem.

PATIENT: You have?

DOCTOR: Yes. If I could talk the next patient into landing at La Guardia next week instead of the Skyport, we wouldn't have to cross mid-town to get you home from work. We could take the Lincoln Tunnel on the way to Jersey City, drop you off, and then take the George Washington Bridge on the way back!

PATIENT: But this doesn't have anything to do with my—

DOCTOR: Or better yet, we could take the Holland Tunnel back, since hardly anyone is driving into Manhattan at this time of day, then hook up with the Long Island Expressway and switch over to the Van Wyck Expressway all the way to La Guardia!

PATIENT: I really wish we could focus a bit more on my—

DOCTOR: Hand me that walkie-talkie.

PATIENT *(glumly):* There's something I should probably tell you, Doctor.

DOCTOR *(agitated):* What is it? Speak up.

PATIENT: Two lanes of the Van Wyck Expressway are closed for the next six weeks.

DOCTOR: Do you know this for sure?

PATIENT *(reaching for another tissue):* Yes.

DOCTOR: I hate this town and everyone in it.

PATIENT *(handing the tissue to the doctor):* You've got to try to relax.

IT'S A MATTER OF OPINION

In a poll conducted in the fall of 1993, only thirty percent of the citizens of France indicated they were in favour of the idea of creating a national holiday for pets. This stunning result was obtained in one of the thousand or so national polls conducted annually in that highly opinionated country. The French are so fond of opinion polls that no one there, to my knowledge, has ever bothered to conduct an official opinion poll to determine the public's opinion on official opinion polls.

I'm not sure whether the average Canadian would even agree to respond to a poll on the feasibility of a statutory holiday for pets, let alone how individual preferences might break down if they did answer it. For the record, I'm not in favour of a national holiday for pets. I believe pets, for the most part, presume they are on a life-long holiday. To enshrine their right to an official day off in the constitution would only confuse them. Besides, what would the average dog or cat do on its day off that it doesn't already do on its days on?

The French— thirty percent of them, at least — hold a diametrically opposed view on this subject. But then, it's worth recalling that the French revere poodles and Mickey Rourke.

When you're conducting national opinion polls at the rate of almost three per day, as is the case in France, you soon exhaust the traditional political topics such as how people might feel about reinstating the guillotine, or if Parisians are truly superior to everyone else in the world, as they seem to believe. One hotly debated French poll asked citizens whether they dunked their bread in their morning coffee, and if so, whether they felt free to perform this act in public. The results of the poll showed that sixty-seven percent of Frenchmen dunk their buttered *tartine* in their coffee, and sixty-two percent of these dunkers openly do so in public. But only fifty-eight percent of Frenchwomen admitted they dunked at all, let alone in public.

A possible similar poll in Canada might ask citizens if they break off a piece of their doughnut with their hands before eating it, or if they simply clamp their jaw down on the entire doughnut. But I suspect most Canadians wouldn't condescend to answer such a personal question. The French are passionate navel-gazers with an abiding interest in the tiniest details of their national character and sensibilities. Canadians, on the other hand, are navel-gazers only to the extent that they want to make sure there isn't any lint in it.

The sixteenth-century Italian political philosopher Machiavelli, whose ideas were so cunning and devious that we call cunning and devious persons "Machiavellian", is considered the father of the opinion poll. Apparently Machiavelli was one of the first politicians in all of recorded history to deduce that a good way of acquiring and retaining power was to understand as clearly as possible the wishes of the people. If Machiavelli were a politician in present-day France, he would be opposed to a national holiday for pets but firmly in favour of dunking bread in coffee.

The first actual opinion poll was conducted during the 1824 presidential election in the United States, when two Pennsylvania newspapers asked their readers to state their political preferences ahead of time. In the early days of newspaper surveys, the idea behind them was to try to speed up the reporting of election returns, which sometimes took weeks. Nowadays, of course, election campaigns throughout the free world consist of an almost daily series of opinion polls which all but nullify the point of the official voting at the end of the campaign. Viewed in this light, the French are perhaps on to something with their polls on pet holidays, bread-dunking and the relative importance of saying "thank you" (ninety-five percent of the French populace believe saying "thank you" is important). Instead of pressuring us into divulging whom we would vote for if an election were held today, opinion polls should explore more thought-provoking issues such as our favourite pasta (mine is rigati), the optimum ply of toilet paper (mine is two-ply, though one-ply is acceptable in wartime and other national emergencies), and our general attitude toward the people of France (mine is cautious optimism).

Given the lightning-fast technology of the information highway now at our disposal, there's no reason we can't eventually ascertain through opinion polls where we stand on everything, including the earth beneath our feet.

(The foregoing opinions are considered accurate nineteen times out of twenty within a margin of error of plus or minus three.)

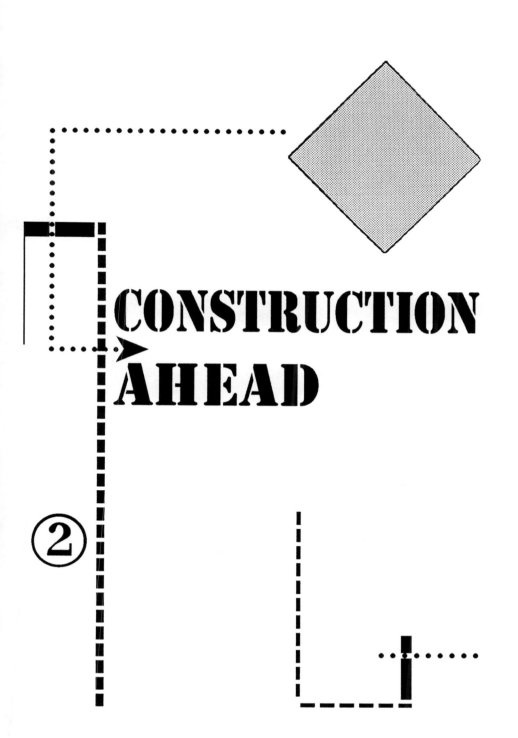

CONSTRUCTION
AHEAD

②

MISSION UNFEASIBLE

The eight-member crew of Biosphere 2, a prototype Martian colony in the Arizona desert, recently emerged from their sealed environment after two years of voluntary isolation. These men and women locked themselves in Biosphere to determine, among other things, if living in a prototype Martian colony for two years would drive them crazy. Apparently it didn't. They strolled out of their elaborate artificial environment looking trim and sane in matching futuristic jumpsuits. If cabin fever was a factor at all in their two-year period of confinement, they weren't letting on.

"I have glimpsed paradise," botanist Linda Leigh remarked to the assembled members of the press shortly after emerging from Biosphere. What we can glean from her statement is that being single and confined with seven other single persons in a well-stocked dwelling with ample food-growing capabilities far from the hurly-burly of contemporary life was not an entirely unpleasant experience.

In some respects, Biosphere 2 sounded more like a prototype twenty-first century Club Med than a prototype Martian colony. I suspect the first men and women who journey to Mars, like the first men and women who do virtually anything, will encounter a number of physical and emotional hardships that never cropped up in Biosphere 2.

Regardless of what they did or didn't have to put up with, the Biosphere crew set a new endurance record for living in a closed system. The previous mark was six months, set by a team from the former Soviet Union. Off the earth, the record is a one-year stay by Russian cosmonauts aboard the Mir space station. (Toronto Blue Jays season-ticket holders don't qualify for the endurance record, since they occasionally leave the sealed environment of SkyDome to go to work, sit in traffic jams and sleep.)

Even more important than the sheer length of time people spend in a sealed, artificial environment is how isolated they feel from the rest of humanity. Biosphere 2, like SkyDome most of the time, was a closed system. But if anything had gone wrong — for example, if the oxygen had become too thin, as happened twice in Biosphere — the residents of the facility knew that help was close at hand. That won't be the case for those intrepid men and women of the twenty-first century who voluntarily strand themselves on Mars. The Arizona desert may be off the beaten track, but the average distance of Mars from Earth is seventy-eight million kilometres. Night-time temperatures there routinely drop as low as -125 Celsius, and the atmosphere is one hundred times more thin than that of Earth. Club Med it isn't.

Systematic testing for cabin fever will be a crucial part of any serious effort to send human beings to other planets. The sheer time it takes to move from place to place in our solar system, let alone between stars in our galaxy or from one galaxy to another, means that future space travellers will inevitably be exploring new frontiers of tedium. Even if we were somehow capable of travelling at the speed of light – three hundred thousand kilometres per second – it would take four and a half years to reach the nearest star, Alpha Centauri. The two years the Biospherans spent cooped up in their Arizona colony represented less than half of a one-way trip to that star, assuming we ever catch up to the speed of light.

Cabin fever is caused not so much by isolation as by a lack of purpose. The simple fact is that human beings thrive on adversity more than they do on comfort. For the past couple of generations, the industrialized world has lived in a state of material comfort unprecedented in history, and the planet itself has paid a high price for that comfort. Humanity would benefit greatly from joining hands in a challenging enterprise such as finding new planets to sully. I'm not saying we would have as easy a time of it as the cast of *Star Trek*, who flit casually from one celestial body to another without due regard for things such as oxygen, gravity and the fact that not everyone in the universe can possibly speak English. But a shared sense of mission has been known to carry people through tremendous adversity.

Preparations for these future space missions may have already begun among the general population. It could be that the recent trend toward a "cocooning" lifestyle, whereby people increasingly confine themselves to their homes, is humanity's unconscious way of steeling itself for endless journeys to the outer limits of space. That often maligned specimen of contemporary life, the couch potato, may unwittingly be in the vanguard of human evolution, helping the human body adapt to the prolonged states of inactivity without which all serious space travel will be impossible.

All in all, the future promises to be an exciting, crushingly boring time.

IN THE VALLEY OF THE APPLIANCES

I religiously stay away from retail establishments during the annual consumer frenzy known as Boxing Day (or Boxing Week, as some zealous merchants have taken to calling it.) I also try to do as little shopping as possible during Advent, when everyone prepares for the birth of Christ by spending money as though the Second Coming were at hand. Shopping displeases me so much that I almost wish a system were in place whereby I could donate fixed amounts of money to various retail outlets in return for the delivery of randomly selected merchandise of commensurate value.

Anguish has been built right into the contemporary shopping experience. Many of the products you purchase today, especially appliances and audio-visual equipment, will have been supplanted by more sophisticated models before you've even finished reading the operating manual. A friend of mine who's keenly aware of this problem has deliberately held off buying a new television for the past five years because he knows even better models are just around the corner. He thinks this is a solution to the problem. All I know is that he's done without a proper working television for the past five years.

"Why should I waste money on an inferior TV when all I have to do is wait a few more months for one of the newer models?" he explained to me.

"You've been telling me that for the past five years," I said to him.

"I know I have."

"So when are you going to buy a new TV?"

"I don't know," he said. "They keep making them better and better. I may never buy one."

This is the inertia that has begun to grip the marketplace – a fear of being swindled by the passage of time.

Not long ago, I went on a rare, angst-ridden shopping expedition for a new kettle. I ventured into an appliance store and was arrested near the door by the soothing sight of vapour emerging soundlessly from the spout of a room humidifier. The clerk moved stealthily from behind the counter in the manner of a cheetah stalking a less fleet-footed creature. To placate him, I half-heartedly expressed an interest in the workings of the humidifier. He told me the unit "pulverized" the water before converting it to vapour, which apparently was a desirable thing. There may also have been something about negative ions in his spiel, though I couldn't say for sure. He said the price of the unit had been drastically reduced because of some minor defect which had since been repaired. He went looking for the operating manual in the storeroom, misled by my civility into believing I might actually want to buy the thing.

While the clerk was rooting around in the storeroom, I gave myself a quick tour of the store. Arrayed on various counters were gleaming, seductive appliances of various sizes and shapes. I recognized a few sleek, European-style toasters which, unlike North American-style toasters, don't function as leg-hold traps for bagels and English muffins. Most of the Euro-toasters had slots wide enough to accommodate even the most ineptly sliced bread. Down a bit from the toasters were the coffee-makers, including a selection of mind-boggling cappuccino machines that seemed to have been designed for the convenience of moderately thirsty leprechauns. I realize that drinking cappuccino is one small step away from intravenous injection of caffeine, but do the machines and the amount of coffee they make have to be so tiny?

Then came the kettles. Hardly any of them were chrome-plated. At some imperceptible point between the last time I bought a kettle and now, chrome had gone out of style. This highly reflective metallic element had been the optimistic mirror on many consumer items in the jolly, money-grows-on-trees post-war era. Now you rarely saw chrome on anything, including automobiles. The colour scheme of the kettles in the store ranged from white to off-white to semi-white to light grey. The kettles looked institutional rather than jolly. It was easy to imagine large urine samples being stored in them. Many of them had little windows and volume indicators through which you could accurately gauge how much liquid had been poured in. The kettles were joylessly utilitarian, and probably halfway to obsolescence as I gazed at them.

In the centre of the store was an island on which the store's most revolutionary appliances were showcased under track lighting. What unsettled me about these appliances was that I had no idea what any of them were for. One looked like a European-style Geiger counter. Perhaps it was a negative ion pulverizer. The appliance next to it looked like a portable nuclear reactor. Maybe it was a pressure cooker. When I was a child, my mother sometimes used a pressure cooker to prepare the family meal. All these years later, I remain entirely unaware of the nature and purpose of a pressure cooker. Perhaps it has something to do with the special cooking properties of un-pulverized steam.

The sight of all this mysterious technology made me feel out of touch and dysfunctional. I realized that even if I were wealthy beyond my wildest dreams, there would still be a long list of esoteric instruments to acquire: guava grinders, pomegranate pitters, artichoke heart surgeons, wham-bam-thank-you-yams, etc. When the clerk returned from the storeroom and said he couldn't find the operating manual for the room humidifier, I thanked him and hurriedly left the store, feeling much the way Dante must have felt when he came up from the depths and saw the stars again.

GRAVE NEW WORLD

Ontario's common sense revolution is rapidly spreading around the world. In Romania, for example, residents are being urged to bring their own shovels to funerals as a way of cutting grave-digging costs and promoting the concept of self-reliance.

I propose taking the Romanian common-sense initiative one step further: Since shouldering one's own burden in life is a desired goal in these times of shrinking economic prospects and ballooning public debt, all citizens should make a point of digging their own grave. That way, they will spare loved ones and friends the labour and expense of digging it on their behalf after they've passed away.

Such a plan would necessarily entail a certain amount of public education, since not everyone knows the optimum width, length and depth of a grave. A round of public seminars by professional grave-diggers could help familiarize citizens with the logistical aspects of digging their own grave, as well as the preferred size and shape of shovel for getting the job done as efficiently as possible.

Some people may feel that digging their own grave is an unduly morbid task, as well as unacceptably menial. This is a natural first response to the idea. But in time, all citizens will see that self-initiated interment preparation is no less an investment in their own future financial security than RRSPs and pension plan contributions.

For too long, the notion of digging one's own grave has been shrouded in disapproval. The common phrase, "You're digging your own grave", instead of signifying a potentially fatal lack of judgment, should mean that a person is demonstrating exemplary initiative and self-reliance. For instance: "That young man has a very bright future ahead of him. He's digging his own grave."

I see the possibility of enjoyable fresh-air celebrations for family and friends centred around a self-initiated interment preparation at the cemetery. As with your first communion, bar mitzvah, graduation, marriage and other milestones of life, digging your own grave could become an occasion for sending out invitations and soliciting small gifts from family members and friends. This way, there would also be the likelihood of some help — or at least practical advice — when the time came to get down to the actual digging.

The shift to self-initiated interment preparation will naturally cause structural upheaval in the funeral industry, including the elimi-nation of some professional grave-digging positions. But I foresee an exciting new consulting role for grave-diggers and funeral directors.

In Romania, coffins on roof racks and even in streetcars are becoming a common sight as citizens do their best to live — and die — within their means. We can only hope that similar images of frugality and self-reliance soon become commonplace on the streets of our own communities. The fact that Romanians have embraced self-im-posed thrift is all the more remarkable when you consider the adjust-ment they have had to make from the Communist mayhem under which they lived for decades to the current free-market mayhem. In

Ontario, citizens have a much less dramatic leap to make to become comfortable with the idea of gradually weaning themselves off government handouts and correcting unrealistic personal spending patterns.

There was a time when the notion of "paying your own way" was an emblem of pride and self-esteem. That notion was rooted in the rugged philosophy of the pioneers who toiled so hard to open up this country. But it has been eroded over a number of generations by the insidious idea that we could help one another. The administrative costs alone of helping one another has far outweighed any of the potential benefits.

We have arrived at a turning point in the economic life of the country. Only with courage and imagination can the present crisis be overcome. Instead of bemoaning the end of an outmoded economic system based on sharing, let's seize the opportunities for growth and self-fulfilment represented by the new system based purely on the fruits of one's own labour.

The time has come to follow Romania's example, to lash the coffins of loved ones to roof racks and drive boldly into the twenty-first century. The time has come to stand up and say: "I believe in doing it myself. From this day forward, I'm digging my own grave."

NEW FRONTIERS OF FOOD

I have a feeling the rejuvenation of frozen meals in recent years is due mainly to the fact that the manufacturers of them have succeeded in getting us to stop calling them TV dinners. In our household, we no longer have a commonly accepted term for prefabricated frozen dinners. The other day, when my wife used the words "TV dinner", I had to pause awhile before I understood what she was alluding to. Rather than the tastefully designed, calorie- and cholesterol-reduced frozen food products of today, she was alluding to a rectangular serving of salisbury steak, with a small side-order of mashed potatoes in a little compartment of its own on the flimsy aluminum serving tray, next to the fluorescent serving of peas, two or three of which invariably strayed into the even smaller compartment with the pudding-like dessert substance in it. She was alluding to the act of pretending to enjoy this ersatz steak dinner while watching an episode of *My Three Sons* or a half-hour of Don Messer and his Islanders on the television, which was probably black and white with ineffectual rabbit ears atop it.

In recent years, as the makers of TV dinners began to pursue a wider share of the groceries market, they played down the TV-watching angle of the meals they manufactured in favour of the convenience and nutritional properties of their product. This change in advertising strategy had minimal impact on me, since I was one of those who genuinely appreciated TV dinners for what they were: a kind of science-fiction notion of what food might be like in the distant future, when people no longer have any idea of what things are supposed to taste like.

It was this futuristic aspect of the whole TV dinner experience that captured my youthful imagination. Everyone knew the American astronauts of the period ingested Tang flavour crystals when they were in space. In all likelihood they also sucked on TV dinners with the neatly compartmentalized entrées, the easily disposable containers and the cheerfully bland simulations of actual food inside them. To eat a TV dinner in those days was to accept membership in the great human community of the looming twenty-first century. At least that's how it felt to me each time I peeled away the foil cover and beheld a steaming clump of slate-coloured salisbury steak wallowing in a kind of sauce.

When TV dinners first came on the scene, the notion of being pressed for time was not as deeply embedded in our collective psyche as it is today. The occasional TV dinner was considered a special treat to be slowly savoured rather than the necessary consequence of an overlong work day, three hours of commuting and a time-management seminar in the evening. In the salad days of my youth, I savoured the clump of salisbury steak the way a wine connoisseur might slosh a fine vintage in her mouth. Sometimes, perhaps because of an error in operating the oven, not all of the salisbury steak I savoured was piping hot – or "unthawed", as we quaintly put it in those days. But this, too, was accepted as part of the risk of participating in the great experiment of space-age living. Nowadays, of course, people rarely have time to heat TV dinners in a conventional oven. A microwave oven can irradiate frozen food molecules to an acceptable serving temperature in a fraction of the time it used to take back in the time when we had more time.

Today's high-definition TV dinners are marketed in modular components more often than not, which is a fancy way of saying you have to buy a separate package of frozen spinach to go with the package of chicken Kiev instead of relying on the everything-in-one concept of the past. One possible reason for this innovation is that by selecting combinations of pre-manufactured frozen food, consumers are made to feel that they're "preparing" their dinner the same way their parents and countless generations before them prepared dinner. Just because preparing one of these dinners involves no labour of any kind doesn't mean we can't feel a profound connection with our forebears as we wait for the beep of the microwave to call us to the table.

A VIRTUAL REALITY CHECK

I wasn't surprised to learn that a lot of people who play around with virtual-reality technology suffer motion sickness, disorientation and vivid flashbacks. Actual reality is hard enough to negotiate without bamboozling the brain and central nervous system with electronic imitations of it.

What I was surprised to learn, though, was that the people involved in the research and development of virtual reality were surprised. They seemed especially chagrined by the fact that a high proportion of the equipment's target market, teenagers, become sick to their stomach after donning virtual-reality headgear and spending some time in a computer's model of the world.

Elementary logic dictates that virtual reality will almost always be more sick-making than reality. If a certain percentage of people throw up while aboard a ferris wheel because of the vertigo caused by the motion of the ride, it stands to reason that a virtual-reality simulation of a ferris wheel will cause even more people to throw up. This is because of the additional adjustments the body must make when it experiences virtual reality. On a real ferris wheel, the rider must adjust to the bobbing and vertical rotating motion of the ride, and to the fact that it's being operated by an unsavoury gentleman in grease-caked overalls. On a virtual-reality ferris wheel, the rider must adjust to the bobbing and rotating motion of the ride while sitting motionless in a little room, and to the fact that the ride is controlled by an unsavoury gentleman with an assortment of pens in the breast pocket of his smock.

I've ridden a few roller-coasters in my time, including a hair-raising simulated bobsled run down a replica of the Matterhorn at Disneyland several years ago, when my body and mind were more receptive to stimuli of that kind. But by far the most terrifying roller coaster ride I ever took was while seated safely in the IMAX theatre at Ontario Place. The filmed version of the ride was so vivid and over-whelming that my brain was unable to convince my body that it wasn't about to be thrown from the theatre seat to some grotesque facsimile of sudden death.

Frankly, I've been suspicious of virtual reality ever since it reared its ugly simulation of a head. So far, the only serious justification of this technology has been that it can help human beings learn complex operations, such as piloting a jet aircraft, performing surgery or setting the clock on their VCR. But now even these practical applications have been called into question. Consider the real-life experience of a University of North Carolina psychologist who spent twenty minutes wearing a virtual-reality headset and watching a program designed to show surgeons how organs and muscles look inside the human body. When she took off the headset, the psychologist reached for a soft drink and proceeded to pour it into her eyes. Other users of virtual-reality programs have reported that when they remove the headset, the real world looks upside down to them and people seem to be walking on the ceiling. And a pilot who trained on a virtual-reality simulator said he had to pull his car over the following day because he had a vivid flashback and suddenly thought he was driving on an electronic road.

What these experiences imply is that the human body doesn't take kindly to being made to look foolish. While wearing the virtual-reality headgear, your mind may be perfectly aware of the fact that nothing is real, but your body isn't and it doesn't appreciate the joke.

Reality, as we know it, can be a difficult thing with which to remain in contact for prolonged periods. It could be argued that much of contemporary life amounts to attempts of various kinds to divorce ourselves from reality. On the other hand, some philosophers and physicists claim there is no such thing as objective reality, in which case we're all wearing virtual-reality headsets whether we realize it or not. Whatever the case, the simple fact is we really don't need any more realities than we already have.

Reports of widespread sickness have been a major setback to the virtual-reality industry's efforts to capture a piece of the lucrative video-game market. Probably the cruellest irony of all is that people fifty years of age and over show no symptoms of sickness or disorientation after using virtual reality. But nor are they much interested in using it. From age fifty onward, most people tend to feel the real world is virtual enough, thank you very much.

REST AREA

③

A CLUSTER ANALYSIS OF TIME-KILLING STRATEGIES

Before social scientists can adequately study and pass judgment on our leisure habits, they must do what all good scientists do before they do anything else: They must define terms, establish parameters, assemble frameworks, calibrate models, apply for fellowships and answer fan mail.

One of the terms social scientists have managed to define is "leisure", which they interpret as a measure of time rather than a description of someone sitting on a lawn chair. For their purposes, leisure is the remainder of time after work, sleep and personal and household chores have been completed.

The Protestant work ethic, which for some reason has not fallen entirely out of favour, is based on the philosophy that work is the primary purpose of life. The role of leisure within the Protestant work ethic is that of preparing an individual for work through exercise (preferably brisk and unpleasant) or relaxation (preferably brief and guilt-ridden). As far as I know, there is no such thing as a Catholic work ethic – or a Muslim, Buddhist, Hindu, Shinto or Zoroastrian work ethic. Only Protestants have dared to align their faith so intimately with the notion of drudgery as a virtue.

On the far side of the sociological spectrum from the Protestant work ethic are the hedonists, who govern their lives by a kind of ecumenical party ethic. This ethic has been steadily gaining ground on the Protestant work ethic in recent years. As a result, the scientific community has sharpened its focus on the recreational aspects of daily life. A cursory examination of the titles of bona fide academic studies in recent years shows the breathtaking range of their research. I refer you to such ground-breaking treatises as:

* *Specialization, Displacement and Definition of Depreciative Behaviour Among Virginia Canoeists* (U.S.Department of Agriculture Forest Service, 1980).

* *The Role of Gender, Motivation and Clubhouse Access on the Total Sports Experience* (University of Victoria, 1984).

* *A Cluster Analysis of Activity, Frequency, and Environmental Variables to Identify Water-Based Recreation Types* (Journal of Leisure Research, 1975).

* *The Social Construction of Unreality: An Interactionist Approach to the Tourist's Cognition of Environment* (Humanistic Geography, 1978).

These and other studies are shedding new light on our leisure-time behaviour, as well as opening up whole new vistas for academics and bureaucrats to explore in a gainful and time-consuming manner.

However you measure it, the world of recreation is a growth industry. Statistical research over the past quarter-century shows a steadily rising curve of public participation in virtually all leisure activities. But this doesn't mean everyone is happy with the way they're spending their free time. For instance, a 1984 study asked residents of the province of Alberta to list their leisure-time activities according to participation, frequency of participation and personal preference. Of the thirty-three leisure activities listed in the study, watching television placed first in terms of both overall participation rate (ninety-four percent) and most frequent participation (seventy-eight percent). But it placed only eleventh (three percent) in the list of preferred activities. What this means is that a lot of Albertans are sitting through episodes of *Baywatch* more or less against their will.

Social scientists have isolated five principal factors that contribute to the setting of realistic leisure-time goals. By measuring your own personal circumstances against these six factors, you can more accurately determine what you should be doing in your spare time.

1. **Available leisure time**. This factor is so self-evident that I almost didn't include it. Undoubtedly, the amount of leisure time at one's disposal will affect the nature and extent of one's leisure-time activities. For example, the average factory worker won't have as much time to kill as a professional athlete or bureaucrat. A factory worker might only have time for a stroll to the corner store for cigarettes, whereas professional athletes or bureaucrats might sail to the Azores on a fully-equipped schooner for their cigarettes.

2. **Income**. All paycheques are not created equal. This has direct ramifications upon a person's leisure lifestyle. The reason Hollywood stars flock to swanky resorts such as Aspen, Colorado is not simply because Hollywood stars prefer the company of people with similar hairstyles, wardrobes and personality disorders. They go there to get as far away as possible from people like you and me, who would need

a mortgage to pay the lift fees at Aspen. Wealthy people don't have to worry about making ends meet. Their ends are forever being introduced to one another.

3. **Education**. Studies show that university graduates play horseshoes less frequently than high-school dropouts. University graduates don't know what they're missing.

4. **Age**. This is less of a factor in leisure-time choices now than in the past. Society's "mature sector" is becoming more healthy, active and foolhardy than ever before.

5. **Sex**. You're more likely to be interested in participating in leisure activities which involve it.

While measuring these five factors, try to disregard spurious statistical analyses that would have you believe everyone in your neighbourhood has successfully climbed the Matterhorn and is learning Sanskrit through the mail. By and large, your neighbours are as unsure as you are of how best to exploit their leisure time.

As the Bhagavad Gita instructs: "On action alone be thy interest, never on its fruits." In other words, it doesn't really matter whether you're white-water rafting down the Yangtze River or playing Yahtze with your children. The point is you're going to be doing a whole lot more of it in the years to come.

A SEASON AT MERCIFUL ACRES

1: The Honeymoon

Although I haven't played the game in more than twenty years, I need only look down at the little white ball resting patiently on its little tee to understand the primordial allure of golf. That ball represents more than just the promise of a breathtakingly sweet drive to within putting distance of the cup. As I gaze fondly down at it on this bright June morning, the ball seems to symbolize my future as a whole — perhaps the future of all humanity. It is the seemingly modest sphere into which untold generations have poured their fondest dreams for their children, their children's children, and their children's children's—

"Are you going to hit the ball or what?" my partner interjects.

It's not an unreasonable question, given that I've been standing over the ball for several minutes. A foursome of retirees, resplendent in pastels and canary yellow, is grumbling just a few yards back of us. Their patience, like the mist that blanketed the fairway at dawn, has gradually burned away. They feel that a person such as me, in the comparative prime of life, has no business impeding their progress through the twilight of their own. They are here at Merciful Acres Golf & Country Club for the same reason I am. But they would never dream of loitering for such a long time over a tee shot. In others words, they have a much better idea of what playing golf entails than I do.

I am one of a growing number of citizens who, seemingly commanded by divine forces, have decided to re-familiarize themselves with golf as a way of smoothing their passage from their peak-earning years to their early-retirement-buyout years. After eons away from the game, I've instantly fallen back in love with it. But I'm suffering from the proverbial first-date jitters: I don't know whether to shake hands, kiss, or blindly feel my way around.

The clubs I'm using were given to me by my mother after she retired from the game. My partner, who similarly has been away from a golf course for some time, is also using his mother's equipment. I've decided I can't afford to choke up on the three-iron I'm using on the first tee because my mother is shorter than I am, therefore her clubs must be shorter, too. Then again, I'm not sure if I'm supposed to choke up on the club even if it's a full-length man's club. Obviously, I have a lot of catching up to do.

Address the ball is a piece of advice I recall from my youth, so that's what I do. I pull the club back, the ball and tee quiver in anticipation, I keep my head down and whip the club forward. The impact of the clubhead on the ball produces a supremely satisfying THWACK!, just like on television. I have no idea where the ball has gone but I instinctively peer due south, to where the green is.

"Where did it go?" I ask my partner after an appropriate period of time. He points due west, to where the traffic on the highway is.

As played on TV by masters in florid trousers, their bronze foreheads crowned by bright visors embossed with brand-name advertisements, golf seems a heavenly blend of pastoral relaxation and rigorous self-discipline. The players on TV rarely hit a ball onto a busy highway or eight-putt a green, both of which I managed to do on the first hole at Merciful Acres. (When my fifth putt rolled ten feet past the cup, my partner graciously allowed the foursome behind us to play through. That gave me a valuable opportunity to regroup mentally for those crucial final three putts.)

To a degree, playing golf is like riding a bicycle. For instance, you don't forget the essential points of how to grip the club – though you do tend to forget what club to grip and when. Just as no one in her right mind would consider joining the Tour de France after twenty years away from bicycles, a certain amount of remedial training is necessary before a person can get back into the swing of golf. My partner, who has played on three or four occasions since Neil Armstrong walked on the moon, helpfully pointed out that teeing up your second shot is not considered good form. Nor is using your pitching wedge on the green, even if your ball is fifteen or more yards from the cup. He also instinctively knows that if your tee shot dribbles along the ground for forty or even fifty yards in the general direction of the hole, this is not something of which you should be unduly proud.

"You're taking your eye off the ball," he informs me after one such shot. "You're probably expecting to make a great drive and you want to see it take off, so you look up too soon."

"Which eye am I taking off the ball?" I ask my partner.

"Both of them, at the same time."

I sigh and explain to him that my head seems to have a mind of its own.

As the breezy June day lazily unfolds, my game unravels along with it. I launch my tee shot on the ninth hole. My partner and I scan the sky for a considerable time, then we hear the ball return to earth about twenty yards to our left. I have hit the first pop-fly in the history of golf.

"It's miraculous how few strokes it actually takes to get a little ball from here all the way to that little cup over there." I mention this to my partner while sheathing my driver with an entirely inappropriate sense of satisfaction.

Our day at Merciful Acres has reminded me that the addictive ingredient in golf is the eternal promise of a sublime shot, when the peculiarities of body language, mental state, physics, meteorology, dumb luck and destiny magically combine to transform you into someone worthy of washing Greg Norman's balls. I had one such shot with a nine-iron on the twelfth hole. I was about seventy yards from the cup and an even greater distance from any onlooker. I took a natural, relaxed swing and lofted the ball to within three or four feet of the cup.

"Beautiful!" my partner cried from the other side of the fairway.

It was only after we had sunk our respective putts and I was radiant as a bride that we noticed the flag on the pin said 13, not 12.

Evidently the dog-leg on the twelfth hole at Merciful Acres goes right, not left.

2: Reality Sets In

The official slogan of the Merciful Acres Golf & Country Club goes a long way toward explaining the club's name. Its slogan is: OUR FAIRWAYS ARE AS WIDE AS THEY ARE LONG. The guiding philosophy of the club is to provide a hassle-free environment in which golfers can excel at the game regardless of whether or not they're excellent golfers. Most club members consider this philosophy a definite asset, but I'm not so sure.

There have been many times this season when I would have preferred to give up my ball for lost in the woods and take the regulation penalty stroke rather than trudge sideways across yet another treeless fairway in pursuit of a vicious hook that has left me farther away from the hole than when I was on the tee. The reason my short game isn't short is that I'm rarely close enough to the green to practise that aspect of golf. The course at Merciful Acres accommodates my most errant drives. Even if my tee shot travels at a right angle to the hole, I'm almost guaranteed a good lie in someone else's fairway. I find this kind of mercy psychologically punishing.

(For the benefit of newcomers to the sport, a "lie" in golf is the condition of the ground on which your ball has come to rest. If your ball has come to rest in the middle of a swamp, you have what's known as a "bad lie". If you ignore the ball in the swamp, surreptitiously remove another ball from your bag, place it on the fairway and yell to your partner, "I found my ball! It wasn't in the swamp after all!", you are telling a bad lie about your "bad lie".)

"Which hole are you supposed to be on?" a fellow golfer inquires of me after a particularly erratic drive on a hot afternoon in July.

"One of the ones back over there," I mutter.

"You might want to consider moving your left foot a couple of inches closer to the ball," the fellow golfer says as I stand over my second shot.

You might want to consider taking a hike, I think to myself as I flail at the ball with my five-iron, leaving myself a third shot about twenty-five yards shorter than my second shot had been.

"Think about that left foot," the fellow golfer advises as I storm away from him and begin mentally preparing for my third shot. My mental preparation consists of looking for a hardwood tree off which to bounce my third shot so that it will strike the fellow golfer a glancing blow in the kneecap. But Merciful Acres is too merciful to furnish me with a suitable tree. All around me is fairway – an ominous desert of hassle-free grass in which to shame myself.

"You seem a bit more uptight today than usual," my partner remarks when we finally converge on the green. He's looking at a twelve-foot putt for par. I'm looking at someone's neck to wring. "Uptight?" I scoff. "Here at Merciful Acres, where the fairways are as wide as they are long? It is to laugh."

"You seem a bit tense."

"Not in the least," I snarl as I attempt to wrestle my pitching wedge from the bag. The sight of the pitching wedge makes me queasy, which is different from tense but produces roughly the same result in terms of the quality of the ensuing golf swing. Tension and queasiness are states of mind the golfer must ward off at all costs. The ideal state of mind for a golfer is to be relaxed yet alert, prudent yet confident, aggressive yet even-tempered, progressive yet conservative, plain yet filter-tipped. This July afternoon, my state of mind is balanced on a razor's edge between rage and fury. I'm harbouring an acute grudge against the Merciful Acres Golf & Country Club. Gone are the innocence and sense of wonder with which I anticipated my drive at the tee. Gone is the childlike hope that I wouldn't slice the ball across four fairways. That childlike hope has been replaced by the adultlike realization that I have indeed sliced the ball across four fairways. Plus my trousers are starting to split at the crotch. Plus my partner is already on the green. Plus my hairline is receding, and there's a hole in the ozone layer over Antarctica.

Eventually, in the same way geological forces form and flatten mountain ranges, I reach the green. I gratefully put my pitching wedge away and queasily tug on my putter. I'm facing an eighteen-footer for quintuple bogey. The pressure is palpable. I wonder what Fred Couples would do in a similar situation. Then it dawns on me that Fred Couples is never in a similar situation. Golfers with talent have an easy time of it. Not for them the bitter "cure" of convalescent courses such as Merciful Acres. They're too busy grinning and waving their putter at the adoring gallery on sexy championship courses in faraway places.

None of it is fair. Plus, if I crouch to size up the green, my pants will split wide open. This is why my short game isn't.

PARANORMAL SPORTS

1: Anglers of the Round Table

By a process almost as mysterious as the construction of the ancient monument at Stonehenge, I have become an official member of the North American Fishing Club. Notification of my new status arrived in the mail. The notification was printed on the envelope itself for all to see. This struck me as odd, since the message on the envelope instructed me in large block letters to "Please keep what you learn here to yourself, use your special Member privileges for YOUR fishing only – and keep any FREE FISHING GEAR given to you by the Club out of the hands of non-members."

My razor-sharp instincts told me that the message on the envelope to keep what I learn to myself was in fact intended for the eyes of everyone but me, so that they would wish to become an official member of the North American Fishing Club as I had just become. But then it occurred to me that I hadn't fished since I was a teenager, and that when I did fish when I was teenager, I found the activity more or less equal to staring at a wall in terms of overall stimulation. So why on earth had my membership been "approved" in the North American Fishing Club? It wasn't as though I had ever applied for the position. I opened the envelope in the hope of finding out.

PLEASE PLACE THIS CARD IN YOUR WALLET IMMEDIATELY, a blue piece of paper inside the envelope stated. Affixed to the paper was a nifty plastic card with a picture of an angler who looked uncannily like me silhouetted against a pristine evening sky that looked uncannily like the sky over Lake Nipissing, which is the lake on which I discovered that fishing was a lot like staring at a wall. MR. JOHN LEVESQUE was embossed in gold letters at the bottom of the card, next to the words OFFICIAL MEMBER.

Also on the blue piece of paper was the North American Fishing Club's Statement of Conduct, which was a kind of solemn oath. The oath stated that by accepting membership in the North American Fishing Club, "I promise to keep all information, benefits and privileges for use of MEMBERS ONLY, and to maintain the high standards of ethics and observation of fishing regulations which the NAFC represents. I will always be fair and honest in my field test reviews, and I will conduct myself in a courteous and mature fashion while wearing or displaying the Club's insignia. I understand the Club's dues are $2 a month, billed annually."

I didn't understand about the monthly dues, but I was beginning to suspect that I was dealing with a highly organized secret society which for some reason had targeted me as a member. An enclosed letter from the executive director of the Fishing Club provided the key to this revelation. His letter stated that the NAFC is "a round table of North America's best and most dedicated fishermen." The use of the term "round table" was obviously intended to connect the nature and purpose of the North American Fishing Club in my mind with the legends of King Arthur and his fabulous Knights of the Round Table.

My suspicions about the letter's secret code were confirmed when, in the very next sentence, the executive director of the fishing club stated, "From what we know about you, you are our kind of fisherman."

The North American Fishing Club wasn't in the least bit interested in hooking carp from the murky depths of Hamilton Harbour. Instead, the Club apparently had consecrated itself to the age-old quest for the Holy Grail!

But my discovery didn't adequately explain why the NAFC wanted me as a member. Casting around for an explanation, I considered the possibility that the only common characteristic of current and prospective members of the North American Fishing Club was an intense dislike of fishing. Perhaps there was something about our aversion to the sport that uniquely qualified us to become Arthurian knights. For that matter, wasn't a fish the secret symbol of the early Christians?

I haven't entirely decoded the executive director's four-page letter, nor do I know how to operate the membership card, the official membership sticker, or how to implement the fishing club's mysterious statement of conduct. But I do believe I have stumbled upon a secret millennialist movement of potentially enormous importance to the future of the world.

The North American Fishing Club's global plans are transparently set out in one paragraph of the executive director's letter to me. This paragraph states that while most Club members enjoy traditional "fishing methods", some members are "working to develop the techniques, equipment and policies that will define fishermen of the twenty-first century."

It would seem that the North American Fishing Club is preparing for imminent contact either with extra-terrestrials or the lost civilization of Atlantis. I have a gut feeling it's Atlantis, because of the underwater angle.

2: Nostradamus Throws a Curve

Having watched post-season baseball every autumn since I was old enough to focus my eyes on a TV screen, I considered the cancellation of the 1994 World Series an epochal low point in the history of the West. Was I right to feel this way, or should I have got a life and carried on with it? In an effort to answer that question, I decided to consult the writings of one of history's great arbiters of human cataclysms, Nostradamus.

For those who aren't familiar with him, Michel de Nostredame was a physician born in Provence in 1503. Aside from the various bizarre procedures doctors were inclined to perform in those days, Nostradamus fell into the habit of composing verses predicting various catastrophic events from his era to the end of the world, which he scheduled for AD 3797. Legend has it that Nostradamus made his prophetic verses cryptic in order to avoid being branded a magician, since magicians were severely frowned upon in some circles in the sixteenth century. Nostradamus even drafted a disclaimer to accompany his prophecies, thereby displaying the kind of legal acumen that could have earned him a fortune in our century: "Those who read these verses, let them consider with mature mind," he warned. "Let not the profane, vulgar and ignorant be attracted to their study. All Astrologers, Fools and Barbarians draw not near. He who acts otherwise is cursed according to rite."

Although somewhat uncertain of my status in the Fool and Barbarian departments, I nevertheless plunged into Nostradamus' writings in the hope of extracting some mention of the baseball players' strike of 1994. My rationale was that if the strike was worthy of Nostradamus' attention four hundred and fifty years ago, it was worthy of ours today. After several hours of painstaking reading, you can imagine my shock when I happened upon the following lines:

Near the great river, a pit, earth dug out, in fifteen parts the water shall be divided, the city taken, earth, fire, sword, blood, cries, fighting, the greatest part concerns the Colosseum.

After I had decoded Nostradamus' deliberately cryptic wording — not to mention his tortured syntax — the reference to the baseball strike became clear. The key words in this prophecy are "dug out". As every baseball fan knows, the dugout is where the players' benches are located. The fact that the "greatest part" of the cries and fighting "concerns the Colosseum" was a further hint that Nostradamus was prophesying strife in the world of professional sports, in case sixteenth-century readers didn't catch the first "dugout" reference.

The "great river" Nostradamus alludes to could be any of several major waterways that flow close to baseball stadiums: the Mississippi in St. Louis, the Allegheny and Ohio in Pittsburgh, or even the St. Lawrence, which flows not far from Montreal's Olympic Stadium.

Nostradamus' reference to a division into "fifteen parts" is the only inaccuracy in the entire prophecy. During the 1994 season, each of the two major baseball leagues had fourteen teams, not fifteen, in their respective divisions. Perhaps Nostradamus was looking slightly too far into the future, envisioning the leagues after another round of expansion. A minor error such as this can be forgiven.

Having established that Nostradamus foretold the baseball strike, I decided to delve further into his writings to see if I could determine which side he favoured in the dispute — the players or the team owners. Before long, I encountered the following declaration: "An old Cardinal by a young one shall be deceived, and shall see himself out of position."

For years, scholars of the paranormal believed this line referred to the seventeenth-century rivalry between France's Cardinal Richelieu and his twenty-two year-old would-be successor. Only now has it become clear that Nostradamus in fact had baseball in mind when he wrote those words. The "old Cardinal" is Stan Musial, of the St. Louis Cardinals, or any of the players of Mr. Musial's generation whose values had been betrayed by the current members of the Cardinals team, and indeed of all baseball teams.

"Out of position" is a key phrase in this prophecy. It's a term with which every fan of baseball is familiar. It means not being in the right place to field the ball properly. Based on that phrase, I feel it's safe to conclude that Nostradamus sided with the team owners in the strike.

If any of this has helped you to form your own opinion about the cancellation of the 1994 World Series, then Nostradamus and I have done our job.

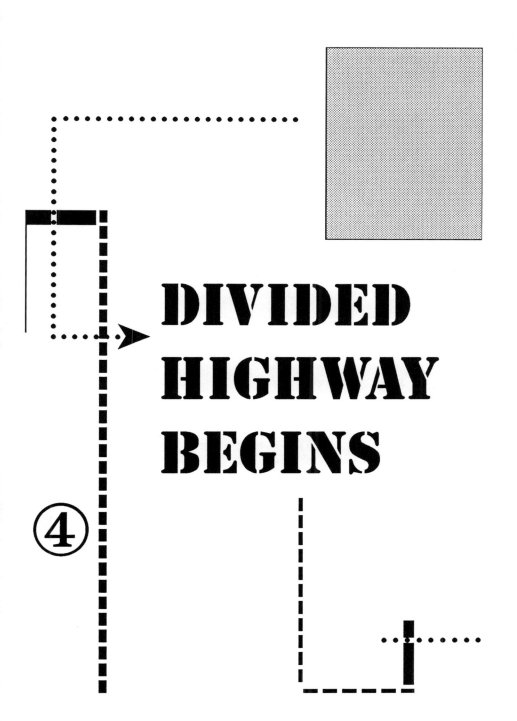

DIVIDED HIGHWAY BEGINS

④

LOVE IS A MANY-SPLINTERED THING

St. Valentine's Day is named in honour of a priest who was clubbed to death and beheaded on February 14, 270 AD. This shows you how much the notion of what's romantic has changed over the years.

The early Christian church decided to use the anniversary of St. Valentine's martyrdom as a way to upstage the old Roman fertility festival of Lupercalia, which was held in the middle of February. Lupercalia was a fairly tame fertility festival by pagan standards. One of its ceremonies consisted of placing girls' names in a box and having each of the boys draw a name. The boy was paired off until the next Lupercalia with the girl whose name he drew. In an effort to alter the general thrust of the ceremony, the early Christian church put the names of saints instead of girls in the box, and the boys who drew the names were supposed to model themselves after the saint whose name they drew. For example, if a boy drew the name of St. Valentine, he was expected to behave in a manner suitable to being clubbed to death and beheaded by pagans. But eventually everyone tired of this game, girls' names were put back in the box, and the martyred St. Valentine became the patron saint of engaged couples.

Valentine's Day is traditionally set aside for expressions of romantic love, as opposed to other kinds of love, such as love of country or love of peanut butter and jam sandwiches. Yet romantic love is a fairly recent innovation compared to these other forms of love. It wasn't until the late Middle Ages, when people in Europe began to tire of their medieval lifestyle in general, that the concept of romantic love came into vogue. You've likely been exposed to the first stirrings of this love in old *Ivanhoe* reruns on television and other fictional treatments of the period, when noblemen proudly wore the colours of their fair maiden while jousting or participating in other uniquely medieval tests of manhood, such as walking in a suit of armour.

Most observers place the origin of romantic love in the twelfth century, when certain French and German noblemen took it upon themselves to set their feelings about personal attraction into verse. Prior to that time, love was seen mainly as a biological urge — what

Joseph Campbell once termed "the zeal of the organs for each other", a kind of impersonal lust about which it might be hard to compose a suitably dignified greeting card, let alone an epic poem. In those early days of romance, marriages were customarily negotiated by the family and ratified by the church. The notion that love could be a spontaneous emotion triggered by the mere meeting of two persons' eyes, regardless of what either of them stood to gain materially from the meeting, was considered the height of frivolity and potentially demonic. Yet the notion of love as something that springs unbidden from the deepest part of oneself has persisted in the West. To most of us in this part of the world, a marriage born of mystical fellow-feeling, with a dash of ageless "organ zeal" thrown in, is a far more valuable affirmation of life than a pre-arranged betrothal that packs all the emotional and spiritual punch of a corporate merger.

Proving one's love is more of a problem in our uncertain age than in the twelfth century, when love was still a novelty. In that chivalrous period, a man was sized up by a woman according to his willingness and ability to suffer things for love, such as the prospect of becoming impaled on the business end of a jousting lance. Nowadays, with so many varied and confusing signals as to what constitutes an appropriate and politically correct expression of romantic love, the heart must somehow guide itself. Can we still love in the same way when we're no longer sure of who we are, and why we're supposed to be in love, and what love is, and which brand of breath mint to use? I certainly hope so.

One twelfth century troubadour conceived of love as an impulse that reached the heart through the eyes. (This should not be confused with the way Sharon Stone looked into Michael Douglas' eyes in the movie *Basic Instinct*. That kind of look was intended to send an impulse to an entirely different part of his anatomy.) What the troubadour had in mind was a system whereby the eyes acted as advance scouts for the heart: "And when they are in full accord and firm in the one resolve, at that time perfect love is born from what the eyes have made welcome to the heart."

The twelfth century abounded in tales of lovers, most of them star-crossed, who defied the conventions of the day, eloped together and died in each other's arms soon afterward. Seven hundred years later, through thick and thin, we cherish these stories because, unlike the characters in them, we have never died in anyone's arms.

MR. CONGENIALITY

The gender equality gap continues to shrink in a number of important ways. The most recent example of this trend is the case of a Virginia woman who won her job back after being unfairly fired for having a moustache.

There's no reason in the world a woman with a moustache can't carry out her work duties just as effectively as a woman without a moustache. In this day and age, it's hard to conceive that something as innocuous as a moustache could have a bearing on a woman's work evaluation. Yet the woman in question and her supervisor were both fired from their jobs at the Ritz-Carlton Hotel in Tysons Corner, Virginia. (The woman lost her job because of her moustache. Her supervisor lost his job because he refused to order the woman to get rid of her moustache.)

Both fired employees filed a complaint with the U.S. Equal Employment Opportunity Commission, claiming they had been wrongfully dismissed. That complaint resulted in a change in heart on the part of the manager of the Ritz-Carlton. He said he was "profoundly sorry" that the incident ever occurred and offered them back their jobs.

This case amounts to an important victory for all women with moustaches, and possibly even for those with underarm hair. It sets an unofficial precedent, in the U.S. at least, that discourages discrimination in the workplace based on having hair in non-traditional parts of the anatomy. If society so easily tolerates the spectacle of men who on a daily basis shave perfectly natural hair growth from their face, there's no reason why society can't also tolerate women who, for one reason or another, don't shave.

The Virginia case reminded me of the similarly progressive resolution of a gender-related dispute in Australia a few months ago. That case revolved around a twenty-four year-old man in a town called Tweed Heads who defeated several women in a local beauty pageant.

Damian Taylor, a hotel worker and part-time lifeguard, competed against the women in the categories of fund-rasing, deportment, personality and knowledge. (There was no swimsuit competition.)

Some of the female also-rans in Tweed Heads were upset that Mr. Taylor stole the limelight from them. But imagine how the organizers of the Miss Australia pageant felt when they learned that Mr. Taylor intended to compete in their pageant, as well. His decision conjured the frightening spectre of a man actually being crowned Miss Australia. This would have sent shock waves all the way to the Miss Universe pageant and perhaps beyond, into other dimensions of time and space.

To head off a possible human rights complaint, the organizers of the Miss Australia pageant decided Mr. Taylor would be allowed to compete in their pageant, but he would not be allowed to win. Thus Mr. Taylor became the first fully sanctioned topless entrant in a beauty pageant swimsuit competition, and the cause of gender equality advanced another step. For too long, beauty pageants have been the exclusive preserve of young women with long legs and more than the regulation number of teeth. By opening the door to a man – albeit a part-time lifeguard – organizers of the Miss Australia pageant acknowledged that beauty, poise, big hair and congeniality do cross the gender barrier from time to time.

Meanwhile, back on the employment front, Statistics Canada reported that the average man's wage declined by 0.4 percent in the 1980s, whereas the average woman's wage increased by fourteen percent in the same period. It's worth bearing in mind, however, that the average woman's wage in Canada is still substantially lower than the average man's wage. But it's also worth bearing in mind that the slight decline in the average male wage in the 1980s was the first such drop since the Great Depression, when work prospects were generally bleak. The rise in women's wages was attributed to their gradual movement into higher-paying senior positions in the workplace. The decline in men's wages was attributed to their gradual movement from the manufacturing sector to the unemployment-insurance sector. In 1991, sixty-one percent of married women in Canada were participating in the labour force. Forty years ago, that figure was eleven percent.

If I had to pull together the various topics I have explored in this piece into a cohesive statement — which I don't have to do, but here goes anyway — I would say this: The challenge facing the average man in the workplace in the 1990s is to learn how to compete effectively against women with moustaches for a dwindling number of beauty pageant jobs.

A FRENCH POSTCARD

The daily mail can be such a dreary thing. If it isn't an unsolicited offer from one of those direct-marketing outfits that are sprouting up everywhere like goldenrod, it's one of a zillion Reader's Digest sweepstakes notifications, or a generic threatening letter from the utility company. So on those rare occasions when a piece of mail arrives at our house with actual human handwriting on it, it's handled with reverence and thankfulness. That's how we felt about the postcard we received from Martin, who was vacationing in the French town of Chalon-sur-Saone, south of Dijon.

"I'm spending a few days in my native town for a bank holiday and everything looks like it used to be," Martin wrote. "I wish you could be here with me to share my happiness."

My wife and I wished the same thing as we looked at the photograph of the half-timbered Maison de Bois on the flipside of the postcard. The Maison de Bois in on the Rue de Pont, near one of the fine quays that flank the Saone River. The town's streets are narrow, the shops look inviting and the sky in the photograph is a tranquil blue.

"I miss you so much!" Martin continued. "I promise to take you to Chalon one day. Good luck for your graduation. I always think about you. I love you. — Martin."

"What a beautiful postcard," my wife sighed.

I couldn't have agreed more. But a part of me nevertheless felt compelled to point out to her that we didn't know anyone named Martin either here or in France, that the postcard was addressed to someone by the name of Roberta, and that it had obviously arrived at our door by mistake.

My wife glared at me over the postcard. "Can't you for once think romantically?"

I believe I can. But like many people, I was subjugated at a tender age by the authority of cold, hard facts. I am the love-child of technology and the scientific method. The first word I spoke as an infant was "Data".

It perhaps is not widely known that the town of Chalon-sur-Saone was an important centre for the tribe of ancient Gauls known as the Aedui. The town was called Cabillonum by the Romans. In the sixth century, it was chosen by King Guntram to be the capital of Burgundy. Hugh IV, Duke of Burgundy, granted the town a charter in 1256. There are a number of fine old houses in the town such as the Maison de Bois on the Rue de Pont in Martin's postcard, as well as a fifteenth-century episcopal palace and the remains of ancient ramparts. Having received a postcard from the town, I considered it my duty to find out that much about Chalon-sur-Saone. Also in the spirit of fact-gathering, I made it my duty to succeed where Canada Post had failed by taking the necessary steps to ensure that the postcard reached Roberta.

Martin had been fairly scrupulous when he addressed and mailed the postcard from France. He had the right name, street number, postal code, province and country. He simply neglected to include the name of the municipality to which the card was to be delivered. In a bizarre compound of initiative and laziness, someone at Canada Post decided Martin got Roberta's postal code wrong, changed it to our postal code in Hamilton and forwarded it to us. It took me less than five minutes with the postal directory at the public library to determine that the postcard should have gone to Port Hope, a manufacturing community on the north shore of Lake Ontario. (The town possesses one of the best-preserved nineteenth-century main streets in Ontario and was originally the site of an Indian village called Cochingomink.) From there, it took less than a minute to consult the Port Hope telephone directory and match the name on the postcard to a specific address in the book. Why no one at Canada Post was able to do this, yet someone went to the trouble of putting a new postal code on the card, is one of those enigmas of human behaviour that can inadvertently set in motion a tragedy of Shakespearean proportions.

For instance, what if Martin and Roberta had quarrelled shortly before Martin went off on his vacation? What if each of them doubted the other's love, and only a tender message could reassure them both that they still cared for one another? Then again, what if their romance was illicit, the postcard was meant to be delivered to a private post office in Port Hope, and I was unwittingly blowing the whistle on Martin and Roberta's sordid affair by forwarding the card to the home of Roberta and her unsuspecting husband, who was known throughout Port Hope for his jealousy, hair-trigger temper and knife collection?

I doubted the latter scenario. Martin struck me as a sincere young man with nothing but pure feelings for Roberta, and Roberta seemed a pleasant and fun-loving young woman who found Martin's courtly, Old World affections exotic and touching.

"How can you possibly know anything about Roberta?" my wife inquired.

"I'm thinking romantically," I told her, my voice quivering with emotion. "These two kids were made for each other. If Roberta doesn't get this postcard, their future together will be in jeopardy."

"So mail the postcard," my wife said.

"I will, will," I said, blowing my nose, taking one last look at the Maison de Bois on the Rue de Pont and Martin's earnest, hopeful handwriting.

By now, Roberta in Port Hope has her precious postcard, Martin's love for her has been reaffirmed, and I'm thinking of offering my services to the federal government as an all-round decent human being.

LET ME CALL ME SWEETHEART

A so-called sexual revolution and a generation of feminism haven't had an appreciable effect on the way men would like women to look and the way women would like men to look.

I don't pretend to be an authority on standards of physical attractiveness a generation ago. In fact, I suspect there were no standards of attractiveness a generation ago; how else to explain the popularity of bell-bottom trousers? But while substantial progress has been made on a number of important gender issues, it seems that men and women cling to the same old physical stereotypes of what turns them on and off. For example, a recent survey of baby-boomer men and women on the topic of physical attractiveness found that women prefer men who don't have love handles and that men prefer women who don't have small breasts. (Love handles, for those men who have never seen or experienced this euphemism, are a gradual enlargement of the male waistline to the point that the hands of a woman who hugs him invariably come to rest on the fleshy mass that spills over his belt.)

The survey found that women of the baby-boom generation also don't care for portly men, which is a polite way to describe men whose love handles have overrun their entire anatomy; nor bald men, whose head perhaps reminds women too much of love handles; nor short men, who probably wish their love handles could somehow grow out of the soles of their feet.

While it would be unthinkable to refer to a woman's breasts as love handles, it's interesting to note that men don't have the same aversion to fleshy protuberances as women do – provided the protuberances occur in carefully designated sections of the female anatomy. Women with large hips or short legs were found to be viewed as less desirable by men. But the survey failed to determine if men felt that women with large hips atop long legs, or small hips atop short legs, somehow managed to cancel out their shortcomings. Similarly, we don't know whether a tall, slim, hirsute man might be in a position to overcome the liability of his love handles.

One area in which there has been a substantial change in the attitudes of the respective genders on physical attractiveness is that of personal body-image. The survey found that a majority of men and women more strongly desire physically attractive bodies for themselves than for their partners. What this finding signifies is that North American sexuality has entered a distinctly narcissistic phase. I'm not suggesting that men have taken to sauntering up to their reflection in full-length mirrors and saying, "Is that a gun in my pocket or am I just happy to see me?" But a certain inwardness has nevertheless crept into contemporary notions of attraction. Perhaps the general feeling is that if one is blessed with a positive physical self-image, this automatically upgrades the image of one's partner, who may not be similarly preoccupied with surface appearances.

It could be argued that in this era of increased personal and political friction between the sexes, physical attractiveness may eventually become the sole determining factor in the perpetuation of the species. In which case, what's to distinguish us from the baboons of northeast Africa who brandish their brightly coloured rear end to potential mates — other than the disconcerting fact that we seem to derive more enjoyment from our own brightly coloured rear end than that of a potential mate?

Beauty of the skin-deep variety has a role to play in society — mainly that of helping to sell cosmetic products and other minor enhancers of self-esteem. But as long as small breasts, baldness, love handles and other distinguishing marks are seen as turn-offs, human beings will be governed by these shallow concerns. If, as seems to be the case, men and women are increasingly falling in love with themselves rather than someone else, let them at least do so for the right reasons.

TRISTAN AND ISOLDE (AN UPDATE)

Tristan pulled into the driveway of the family home after another long day at the Social Sciences and Humanities Research Council of Canada. His plan was to make himself a sandwich, then to settle into his favourite armchair and watch a ball game on television. When he turned the key in the front door, he noticed it wasn't locked. Had Isolde forgotten to lock up before her business trip to Vancouver? He gingerly stepped in and called her name.

"Who's there?" said Isolde in an alarmed voice from upstairs.

"It's me. Tristan."

Isolde appeared at the top of the stairs. "What are you doing here?"

"I thought you'd be out of town by now. I figured I'd watch a ball game on the big TV."

"Without clearing it with me first?" Isolde said as she descended the stairs. "That's one of the ground rules we established a month ago when you moved out."

Tristan nodded. "I just figured since you weren't going to be here. . ."

"Well I am here," Isolde said. "My trip was cancelled at the last minute. The whole office travel budget has been slashed. Meanwhile, I see in the paper that you guys in the public sector are still blowing money left and right."

"The Social Sciences and Humanities Research Council?" said Tristan. "I'd hardly call the work we do 'blowing money'."

"For instance," Isolde said as she swept past her husband toward the living room to retrieve the newspaper, "I read that the Council spent ninety-four thousand dollars studying something called. . ." She scanned the article for the exact words. "Something called 'the resolution of unfinished business with a significant other'. What kind of boondoggle is that, Tristan?"

Tristan scratched his forehead and said, "I happen to be in charge of that study."

Tristan let Isolde prattle on about other projects on which the Social Sciences and Humanities Council of Canada was supposedly wasting taxpayers' money. Isolde seemed particularly incensed by his study of unfinished business with a significant other, as well as an admirably cogent sixteen thousand-dollar study by one of his colleagues of attacks on aristocratic behaviour in eighteenth-century Great Britain. Couldn't she see that these were important topics for professionals in his field, and that a thorough investigation of them could result in the establishment of clearer parameters within the framework of the overall context of the total social sciences and humanities picture?

"At least you guys spent only eleven thousand dollars on that study of diet in prehistoric Japan," Isolde said. "But ninety-four grand on unfinished emotional business? Good Lord."

"The work is very time-consuming," Tristan said. "But the practical spinoffs from our study of diet in prehistoric Japan alone have been too numerous to count. The average uninformed person doesn't understand the wealth of important information these studies generate."

"Such as?" said Isolde.

"Well," said Tristan, "for example, did you realize that laundry starch is made from broken rice grain?"

"No," said Isolde. "How much did that kernel of knowledge cost the Canadian taxpayer?"

Tristan resented the redneck, penny-pinching mood of Canadian citizens in recent years, and it especially bothered him that his estranged wife was in the same mood. He realized there were underlying personal issues that probably were fuelling Isolde's sarcasm, but he nevertheless took umbrage at her tirade and decided to watch the ball game on the small TV in his bachelor apartment.

"You can watch the game here," said Isolde. "I've got work to do upstairs tonight."

"I think I'll go anyway," Tristan said.

"Look, Trist, maybe I came on a bit strong about your ninety-four thousand-dollar study of unfinished emotional business with a significant other. Probably what I'm really angry about is the way you always avoid sitting down with me so we can come to some mutual understanding of why our marriage fell apart the way it did."

Tristan glanced at his watch. The ball game would be on in five minutes.

"Tristan?"

"Yes."

"Do you have anything to say about that?"

"I'd rather not talk about it just now," Tristan said as he fished the car keys from his pocket.

"You never want to talk about it," Isolde said.

Tristan realized she was right as he walked to his car. Then again, he had been terribly busy with his ninety-four thousand-dollar study in recent weeks. The reason he was working so hard on the study was to help him get over some of the personal upheaval of his separation from Isolde. In fact, he had significantly expanded the study's terms of reference to keep his mind off the problem for a while. But what was the point of telling any of that to Isolde? She wouldn't understand.

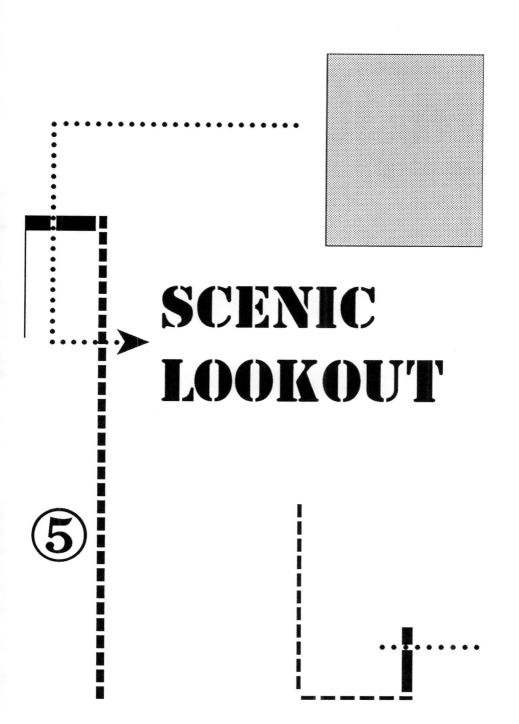

SCENIC LOOKOUT

⑤

A HOME AWAY FROM HOME

Five thousand years ago, a group of Egyptians set out for a mysterious land called Punt in search of incense, gold and dwarfs. This is the first documented case in history of people going on a trip more or less for the hell of it. Unfortunately, no report has come down to us indicating whether these Egyptians located any dwarfs in Punt, or what they might have wanted with them in the first place.

A couple of millennia later, some Phoenicians decided to have a look around the continent of Africa. An admiral named Hanno set sail from Carthage, passed through the Pillars of Hercules in the Strait of Gibraltar and headed down the African coast. Hanno and his men eventually wound up in the Senegal River, where they gawked, not unlike present-day tourists, at the crocodiles and hippopotamuses lolling in the muddy water.

Greece's Odysseus had the first recorded lousy vacation, chronicled at some length by Homer in *The Odyssey*. Homer had a knack for vivid descriptions of exotic destinations that wouldn't have been out of place in a modern-day travel guide. For example: "The immortals will send you to the Elysian plain at the ends of the earth, where fair-haired Rhadamanthys is. There life is supremely easy for men. No snow is there, nor ever heavy winter storms, nor rain, and Ocean is ever sending gusts of the clear-blowing west wind to bring coolness to men."

Homer's effusive description of Rhadamanthys' homeland makes the place seem almost too good to be true. It probably was. The most common disappointment for any traveller, then or now, occurs when out-of-town accommodations don't live up to the advance billing. It could be something as simple as the promise of "whisper-quiet passive air conditioning" at a Caribbean resort, which turns out to be a window. Or it might be a warning embedded in fine print that "hotel rates and surcharges are subject to change without notice", which all but guarantees that the rates and surcharges will change while you have your back turned.

Seasoned travellers are used to the various add-ons — service charges, airport taxes, petty bribes — with which the residents of foreign countries aim to siphon as much hard currency out of visitors as they can. But undoubtedly the greatest potential irritant of any trip is the discovery that the physical accommodations are not what one was led to expect.

In the field of corporate travel, this problem can magnify dramatically. Imagine the logistical headache for a person planning a major business conference in Mexico City when she learns upon arrival in Mexico that the hotel she pre-booked doesn't have a conference room, that the hotel's managers thought she said she needed accommodations for twenty people, not two hundred, that the hotel is in fact a YMCA, that the managers understood the conference was in April of the following year rather than April of this year, and that the YMCA is not in Mexico City at all but in the town of Irapuato, some three hundred kilometres to the northwest.

At least one major American hotel chain is in the process of devising a way to eliminate this kind of unpleasant surprise from a traveller's agenda. James Carreker, president of Wyndham Hotels & Resorts, hopes corporate executives and conference organizers will soon be able to "walk through" a prospective hotel's facilities ahead of time by way of the computer-simulation video system known as virtual reality. What Mr. Carreker has in mind is a program with which prospective users of hotel facilities could "screen" the hotel by "touring" a three-dimensional computer representation of it without actually having to be there to see the actual place.

The idea makes virtual sense. But I do see one potentially major problem with the plan: What's to prevent unscrupulous hotel owners from jazzing up their virtual-reality simulation of their facilities by electronically "installing" luxurious appointments such as "crystal chandeliers" in the "ballroom", "squash courts" on the mezzanine level, and a "safe, sandy beach" across the street from the "ocean-view" rooms? How is the prospective hotel guest to trust the virtual-reality simulation of the hotel any more than she can trust the old-fashioned written descriptions in a more traditional travel folder? For that matter, isn't the traditional travel folder with its sunny verbal descriptions, fanciful sketches and doctored photographs of the hotel's facilities merely a less sophisticated form of virtual reality?

As long as people travel, there will be disappointed travellers: Mini-bars will be understocked, bathwater will be lukewarm, service will be sullen, pork will be underdone. The world is only virtually perfect. A more useful application of virtual-reality technology might be to devise computer programs whereby conventioneers and other travellers can don virtual-reality headgear in the safety and comfort of their own home and imagine they are having a wonderful time attending a conference at a glamorous hotel in some glamorous other part of the world.

All the mysterious lands of Punt – and the incense, gold and dwarfs therein – have been discovered and mapped. All the secluded tropical rivers teeming with ungainly beasts have been charted. Space is the final frontier, but it's not something that can be explored on a long weekend. So let the final frontier be the promise of travelling to fascinating faraway places without stepping out the door.

IN THE ALGOMA TRIANGLE

Somewhere in the dense, nickel-rich wilderness around the city of Sudbury, a paranormal electromagnetic warp in the spacetime continuum is disabling out-of-town automobile parts. My first experience of this strange phenomenon occurred three summers ago, during an otherwise innocuous camping jaunt through north-central Ontario. Late one afternoon, the muffler of our car suddenly broke down on a lonely stretch of highway north of Sudbury. We managed to drive the car into Sudbury, where a muffler specialist who didn't seem at all surprised to see us said we would need a new muffler. We had no choice but to pay him to install one.

Memories of that curious incident resurfaced this past summer when my eldest brother happened to mention that his own car had recently broken down in Sudbury. He was forced to leave his car in that city for a few days and rent another vehicle to get himself home. He told his chilling story as my wife and I were making last-minute preparations for another camping tour of the north. Our destinations this time were Timmins and Elliot Lake. Despite some trepidation in light of my brother's story, we longed for a taste of those patented northern nights when the stars are so brilliant that you can almost hear them through the nylon of the tent. After camping for a few days outside Timmins, our plan was to take Highway 144 down to Sudbury, then to proceed westward along the north channel of Lake Huron to Elliot Lake. About an hour into our drive from Timmins to Sudbury, we noticed a persistent squeaking sound that seemed to be coming from the brakes of the car. I hadn't until that afternoon given much credence to the notion of a kind of automotive Bermuda Triangle in the Sudbury area. But when we came within a dozen or so kilometres of Sudbury and the sound of our brakes had graduated from a squeak to the grinding of metal on metal, I realized that something supernatural was going on.

As far as I can make out at this point, the Algoma Triangle is bounded on the west by Red's Little Hooker Bait and Coffee Shop in Elliot Lake, on the east by Serré's Petro-Canada service station on the Trans-Canada Highway between Warren and Hagar, on the north by the town of Gogama, and on the south by the rather mysteriously named No. 2 Lake. Before you jump to the conclusion that No. 2 Lake is so named because of contamination by raw sewage, it's worth remembering that there are so many lakes in Ontario's hinterland (tens of thousands at last count) that to provide a specific name for each and every one of them is an unrealistic task. Then again, I don't know for sure that raw sewage doesn't leech into No. 2 Lake. And neither my wife nor myself managed to locate a No. 1 Lake in the vicinity of No. 2 Lake. But I'm straying from my central thesis, which is that the Algoma Triangle is a paranormal electromagnetic warp in the spacetime continuum that causes mufflers, brake pads and other automotive parts to go into failure mode.

When any automotive part goes into failure mode, the standard course of action is to perform an on-the-spot failure-mode analysis. I attempted to do this on a gravel shoulder northeast of Sudbury, sandwiched between ominous rock cuts on a darkening Friday afternoon. After figuring out how to open the lid of the hood, I peered in at its contents for a few moments.

"What do you see?" my wife asked from the front passenger seat.

"It's the brakes, all right," I said.

"How can you tell?"

"Well," I said, "there was all that noise they made when I was driving the car."

In due course, a motorist who knew a bit more about automobile failure-mode analysis pulled over and offered to help. I let him drive the car for a spell, after which he agreed with my initial assessment of the problem. As the man gingerly drove our car into the nearby town of Lively for a tow to Sudbury, I asked him if he was aware of supernatural forces in the area that were able to cripple out-of-town automobiles.

"No," the man said, "on account of I'm from Hornepayne."

I glanced over at him. "Then you're at risk, too. Has your car been running okay today?"

"Fine," he said. "She could use a wheel alignment. Other than that. . ."

"What about the muffler?" I asked him.

"Quiet as a church mouse," he said. "No offence, but I don't believe in UFOs and things like that."

"I'm not talking about UFOs," I said. "I'm talking about a paranormal electromagnetic warp in the spacetime continuum. Let me ask you this: Have you been to No. 2 Lake?"

The man cocked an eyebrow in surprise. "The wife and I used a public washroom outside Espanola. We'll be okay 'til we reach Timmins."

"That's not what I mean," I said. "What I mean is —"

"Look, Bud," said the man from Hornepayne, "brake pads naturally wear out. So do mufflers and air filters and fan belts and spark plugs. There's nothing supernatural about any of it."

"But why do I have all my car trouble in and around Sudbury?"

"You don't," the man said. "Your battery froze dead in North Bay last February. And your ventilation fan's gonna go on the bum a few days after you get home from this trip."

I almost accepted the rationalizations of the man from Hornepayne. But he overplayed his hand when he tried to deny the existence of the Algoma Triangle by telling me about car trouble I was going to have in the future. The fact that he was right about our ventilation fan breaking down after we got home from the trip didn't change my mind at all. In fact, it proved that something very strange was going on in the Algoma Triangle.

If you're planning a trip to the area, please exercise the utmost caution. While you're at it, just to be safe, you might want to avoid swimming in No. 2 Lake.

THE PALLOR AND THE TORPOR

The airman-to-airman talks which take place in both formal and informal settings are substantive and have often led to important mutually beneficial decisions regarding our close working relationship.
— From a National Defence press release explaining why Canadian generals were flown at public expense to Florida in the winters of 1993 and 1994 to spend a few days with American generals.

At 0800 hours sharp, an American general began to brief the assembled senior officers from both countries on the day's mission.

"Good morning, men. I probably should begin by explaining how the weather conditions will affect today's sortie. I'm told by my staff that the wind is expected to be thirty knots out of the southeast and the ceiling will be unlimited. This means visibility won't be a problem. But those of you who aren't accustomed to sub-tropical conditions, especially our good friends from Canada, will want to take certain precautionary measures to avoid collateral damage during the mission. Accordingly, I have ordered my staff to make available to each of you small portable canisters of weapons-grade Paba 12 sunscreen lotion which you can take along with you on the mission. Please be sure to apply this substance generously to all exposed parts of the body before we set out."

"Excuse me, General," a Canadian general inquired from amid the group of generals from both countries standing at the foot of a tall palm tree. "Do you have any idea how long this mission might take?"

"I'm glad you asked that," the American general said. "As I'm sure you know, it's often tough to estimate these things ahead of time, bearing in mind the many variables involved in an undertaking of this magnitude and the fact that ground action is hard to predict even at the best of times. Nevertheless, my staff have informed me that we should be in a position to rendezvous back at our temporary HQ on the dining room terrace of Trader Vic's for a debriefing session by 1200 hours. But the top priority, as I'm sure you all agree, is that every element of the mission comes off without a hitch. If that means having to push back the debriefing session into the early afternoon, I'm confident this is a hardship we are all equally willing to bear."

"Thank you," the Canadian general said.

"The wind, as I just mentioned, will be a factor this morning," the American general said. "But I think if we all proceed with an awareness of the effects the wind can have on certain delicate manoeuvres, there's no reason it should seriously impede the sortie. A highly trained and motivated support contingent of ground forces will be on hand at all times to provide logistical assistance and to advise you should any unforeseen problems arise. These men are well-versed in every area of search and rescue operations and, if need be, can provide reliable data on how best to deal with whatever hazards the terrain might throw at us this morning. Besides, I doubt that any of you would have been in favour of scrubbing the mission at this point because of a bit of a breeze."

The generals murmured their agreement.

"I also want to say before we deploy that I was struck by the outstanding esprit de corps all of you displayed yesterday, from happy hour right through to closing time. We all know there's a lot on the line this morning, both in terms of our image as a joint strike force capable of coming together on short notice and because of whatever other stakes may have been established on the outcome of today's action. This could have led to a lot of tension and uneasiness among you last night. Under the circumstances, I thought your behaviour was exemplary. I'm proud of you all."

A Canadian general stepped forward and said, "There's just a bit of mopping up left to do from last night's action. Specifically, there seems to be some lingering confusion about the bar tab and the table-dancer fees."

The American general stood to attention. "The bar tab and table-dancer fees are within our jurisdiction and always have been. As host country of this joint action, we think of last night's ad hoc expenditures as part of the American armed forces' continuing obligation to protect vital interests wherever they arise. As I tell my own staff on a regular basis, we have a duty at all times to be as sensitive as possible to the civilian infrastructure upon which our activities impact. The appropriations issues you raise will be cleared up by the end of the day."

"Thank you for clarifying that," the Canadian general said.

"Unless there are any further questions, I think we should begin the deployment. Please ensure that all your equipment is squared away and that you have adequate ammunition for the entire operation. If you develop a problem with any of the gear, or should any other SNAFU crop up, please ask your unit's aide de camp for assistance. Your aide de camp is there to ensure that you come back safely. There are some men and women in the chain of command who say the general staff have been away from ground operations too long to mount a truly impressive mission on their own. That's why these annual joint winter exercises are so important. We need to demonstrate to everyone from all echelons of the our respective forces that we haven't forgotten what it's like to move on foot through tricky and unfamiliar terrain. As far as I'm concerned, I can't think of anyone I'd rather be heading out with. I mean that."

"I have one final comment," a Canadian general said.

"Fire away," said the American general.

"I just want to say on behalf of all the Canadians here, from the senior officers present this morning to their adjutants, political advisers and publicists back at the Holiday Inn, that we deeply appreciate this opportunity to stand shoulder-to-shoulder with our American counterparts in the shared interest of long-term continental security. I also want to thank you for remembering to inform the chef at Trader Vic's that I'm allergic to shellfish."

"Don't mention it," the American general said. "All right, men. The first tee is just over that ridge. May God go with us all."

TALES OF CELESTIAL BODIES

1

Like thousands of others, we drove away from the city one clear August night to behold the annual Perseid meteor shower from an unobstructed field of view. Like thousands of others, we came home with a stiff neck and a deeper appreciation of the innate bashfulness of the universe. The shower, which wound up being a trickle, was a textbook case of cosmic constipation. When you consider that some eight billion meteors fall into earth's atmosphere per day, seeing a dozen or so in a ninety-minute period hardly qualifies as a life-altering experience.

Scientific PR people were quick to point out that the vast majority of the eight billion meteors that fall into earth's atmosphere on a daily basis are too tiny and faint to be seen by the naked eye. Perhaps this means the Perseid meteor shower is best viewed through a microscope, in which case I wish someone had told us this before we drove into the middle of nowhere to watch it.

A similar celestial letdown occurred in 1986 when Halley's Comet, which passes fairly close to Earth every seventy-six years, last paid a visit. The comet received epic media coverage prior to its arrival, but the arrival itself was a monumental non-event. The best way to simulate how Halley's Comet looked in the night sky in 1986 was to imagine a fly-speck on the lens of your eyeglasses as you gazed up at the stars. The flyspeck was Halley's Comet.

Conditioned as we are by massive fireworks displays on the flimsiest of pretexts – every home victory by the Toronto Blue Jays, for example – it could be that we have come to expect too much from the universe. Perhaps we should be reassured rather than disappointed when the universe fails to give us a spectacular show. Think back to the giant meteor that supposedly fell to earth sixty-five million years ago and caused such a mess that the dinosaurs were wiped out. Is this what we're hankering for in the way of an evening's amusement?

Scientists believe that every century, several meteorites crash into the earth with enough force to produce craters ten metres or more in diameter. On June 30, 1908, a meteor weighing about one hundred thousand tons crashed into central Siberia. Fifteen hundred unsuspecting reindeer were killed, and a man standing on his porch fifty miles away from the impact site was knocked unconscious – or so he said afterward. On the opposite end of the size scale, fifty to a hundred tons of teeny-weeny meteors are said to land on earth every day. Whether we see it or not, we are in the midst of a perpetual meteor shower.

Given these facts, a benign and sometimes boring universe is clearly in our best interests. We should be grateful that the sun burns evenly, that the moon maintains its customary orbit, that the ozone layer is more or less intact, and that large-scale cometary debris mainly stays out in space, where it belongs. Besides, when it comes to deciding what or isn't a spectacular sight, subjective judgments inevitably come into play. For example:

I happened to be on holiday in Cuba in the winter of 1986 when Halley's Comet made its once-in-a-blue-moon flypast through the solar system. One evening that week, the people who ran the hotel in which we were staying had a pig roast. I made a pig of myself and my intestines paid the price. Through most of the night, my body alternated between agonizing gastric pains and Che Guevara's Revenge. Sleep was out of the question. By three in the morning I had worn a visible path between my bed and the toilet. Then, at about four, the spasms finally ended. Euphoric and wide-awake, I wandered outdoors for a stroll in the mild, fragrant night air. On the grounds behind the hotel I spotted a group of people taking turns looking through a telescope mounted on a tripod. One of them motioned for me to join them. "It's the comet," he said. Apparently the pre-dawn hours were the optimum viewing time in that part of the world.

Eventually my turn came to have a look at what Edmund Halley decided in 1705 was the bright celestial object previously witnessed and recorded by astronomers in 1531, 1607 and 1682. Halley predicted the comet would return in 1758. Sure enough, it did – and again in 1834 and 1910.

Through the telescope on that warm and breezy Cuban night, in the calm after my intestinal storm, the faint milky smudge against a velvet backdrop was a wondrous sight. I was in the ideal state of body and mind to apprehend this natural miracle. Here was a distant object, composed mainly of gas, whose movements were as regular as intricate clockwork, or a man's healthy bowels. "Awesome," I said to the assembled stargazers.

I have never forgotten that night, and that night has never forgotten me.

2

Sometimes a single image can crystallize a vast and complicated story more effectively than all the reporting, analysis and panel discussions in the world. A torrent of information often merely produces mud and mildew, whereas the right kind of small symbolic illustration is capable of conveying an intimation of the truth.

Consider the mind-boggling upheaval that rapidly transformed Russia and its neighbouring republics from a decrepit Communist federation into a decrepit capitalist commonwealth. While I can't think of any single story or account that came close to conveying the flavour of everything that transpired in the former Soviet Union in the early 1990s, there is one image in my mind's eye that vividly captures the essence of what happened. That image is of Russian cosmonaut Sergei Krikalev languishing aboard an orbiting space station in the winter of 1992 while his earthbound handlers tried to raise enough money to send someone up to replace him.

Cosmonaut Krikalev probably signed up for the Soviet space program because he had heard it was a glamorous career full of meaningful perks such as a reasonable salary, a multi-room apartment in the city of one's choice, first dibs on quality consumer goods and unparalleled travel opportunities. The Soviet space program undoubtedly had its own version of the American program's notion of physical and emotional superiority commonly known as "the right stuff". Cosmonaut Krikalev must have decided he could do a whole lot worse in life than to aspire to membership in the small heroic elite of pioneers that included Yuri Gagarin, who was the first man to orbit the earth, and several spacefaring chimpanzees who had the "right stuff" more or less forced on them prior to Gagarin's flight. By the end of his mission, Cosmonaut Krikalev would have a much deeper appreciation of the chimps' accomplishment.

After the extensive training all space travellers must undergo, Cosmonaut Krikalev probably felt mildly disillusioned when he was informed that the main purpose of his five-month mission aboard the aging Mir space station was to perform a number of repairs to it. But that disillusion must have paled next to the symphony of emotions Cosmonaut Krikalev experienced when he was informed late in 1991 that his mission aboard Mir was being extended by a further six months because the Soviet space agency couldn't afford to send anyone up to replace him. Add that to the problems with cargo-ship deliveries of food supplies, plus a looming strike by ground controllers and cosmonauts in general, and you would have a fairly accurate idea 8 0   John Levesqueof Cosmonaut Krikalev's mental state at the time if you pictured him as an unhappy space camper.

"Comrade, what goes on?" you can imagine him asking Ground Control over the radio.

"Technical difficulties," you can imagine Ground Control replying. "Please not to call us Comrade anymore. If possible, please not to call us at all."

"Why?" Cosmonaut Krikalev wants to know.

"Much work down here. Talk to you in few weeks."

"But —"

"Fix space station antenna and leave us alone. Please. Over and out."

The main task Cosmonaut Krikalev was ordered to perform when he blasted off in his Soyuz capsule from the Baikonur Cosmodrome in Soviet Central Asia was to fix the space stations's broken antenna. Prior to the launch, Cosmonaut Krikalev repeatedly practised the procedure underwater to simulate the weightlessness of space. He was also instructed to have a look at the space station's onboard computers, which one mission control worker described as "capricious". But fate was far more capricious than any computer. Fate caused Cosmonaut Krikalev's homeland to shatter and more or less reconstitute itself in a matter of weeks while he floated far above the fray, in the uneventful vacuum of earth orbit. Fate condemned Cosmonaut Krikalev to spend another six months stargazing and fretting about oxygen and food while the sweet bluegreen planet drifted lazily under him, oblivious to his condition. The six-month extension wouldn't even break the world record for endurance in space. When his eleven-month mission finally came to an end, it would fall a few weeks short of the record of three hundred and sixty-six days set by another cosmonaut.

In the spring of 1993, when his ground controllers finally found the money to bring him down from orbit, Cosmonaut Krikalev was forbidden to hug anyone for several weeks because of fears that his bones, made brittle by months of weightlessness, would snap. He was also warned that he would have a fatter head for a while, though it hardly could have been swollen by the earthly neglect that left him no choice but to circle the globe again and again, far above the noisy pageant of recent Russian history.

At some point in our life, we're all bound to feel a bit like Cosmonaut Krikalev.

SPEED LIMITS AS POSTED

POISON PEN PALS

In the spring of 1994, Reform Party leader Preston Manning urged Canadians to attach nasty letters to their income tax returns. He said the letters should vividly express the citizens' displeasure with the level of taxation in this country. Mr. Manning obviously has never been the subject of a random income tax audit by Revenue Canada. Had he ever been the target of concentrated scrutiny by this apparatus of the state, he would have thought twice about urging Canadians to be so foolhardy as to append nasty, traceable notes to their income tax forms.

Air-tight anonymity is the key to any written protest against Revenue Canada and its political masters. By all means drop a line to the Prime Minister, the Minister of Finance or the Revenue Minister, indicating to them that you are fed up with the federal system of overspending and overtaxing. Tell them that you're a human being first and a source of public revenue second. But for heaven's sake, do not indicate anywhere in your poison-pen letter your real name, address, telephone number, date of birth, social insurance number, driver's licence registration number, health card number, astrological sign, blood type, or favourite TV program.

In this age of instantaneous computer cross-referencing, there's a risk involved in telling anybody anything about yourself. You never know when someone might file whatever you say into a vast data base for use against you at a later date. For instance, a seemingly innocuous greeting such as, "Enough white stuff for ya?" could be misinterpreted when read several days later from a computer monitor by overzealous federal narcotics agents.

People who are in the business of kidnapping for ransom have a shrewd method of communicating with the people from whom they hope to extract a ransom payment. What the kidnappers do is to painstakingly clip individual letters from magazines, then to painstakingly paste the letters together into the proper order to convey the appropriate ransom message, such as: PAY UP NOW OR KISS THE BUDGIE GOODBYE. The idea behind this tactic is to prevent law-enforcement agencies from tracing the source of the ransom note. In this era of sophisticated police detection, typewriters and computer printers are not sufficiently anonymous tools. While I'm not suggesting that we should in any way condone the actions of persons who ruthlessly kidnap pet budgerigars for personal gain, there's no reason we can't borrow their unique style of letter-writing for the purpose of registering dissatisfaction with the tax system.

Once you have composed your blistering letter to the government (example: I'M SO MAD AT YOU PEOPLE I COULD JUST SPIT!), clip the pertinent letters to form the words you wish to express, paste the letters together on a blank piece of paper, fold the paper and place it in an envelope, take the envelope with you to a foreign country (America is always handy), mail the letter from there with sufficient postage but with no return address on the envelope, then go home and pray that no one is able to trace the letter back to you or any of your loved ones. If you have not become the subject of a random income tax audit within ten years of sending the letter, you're probably safe.

There are additional measures with which Canadians who disapprove of the Canadian tax system can feel more secure about their anonymous hate letter to Ottawa. One such measure is to divert suspicion by attaching a flattering letter of support to your tax return, along with your name, address, date of birth, social insurance number and so on, so that the flattering letter will be electronically cross-referenced as widely as possible. Such a letter of support could read as follows:

Dear Government of Canada,

Just thought I'd drop you a line to let you know what a super job I think you're doing with my money. Please don't allow a minority of nay-sayers in this great land to deter you from the job which you have been elected to do, which is to wrestle the country's finances to the ground. Some people seem to think it's easy. They should try it sometime.

I found your income tax form and the accompanying seven hundred-page booklet very clear and concise this year. Congratulations to the people who worked so long and selflessly to develop such a streamlined system. If, toward the end of the coming fiscal year, you find that you're a bit short, please don't hesitate to contact me for some more money. I'm one of the silent majority of Canadians who believe they are grossly under-taxed.

Earnestly,

YOUR NAME HERE.

Instead of having to send obsequious, signed letters to cover for anonymous hate mail, wouldn't it be nice if a constitutional amendment were enacted whereby the federal government was obliged to hold a general election on April 30 every four years? That way, we could repair to the polling booth immediately after putting our income tax returns in the mail. I can't help feeling this would help to clarify the choices before us.

TOWARD BOSONIC DEGREES OF FREEDOM

Having carefully studied the intricate forty-four page campaign platform of the Natural Law Party, I am now prepared to publicly urge readers to vote for candidates from this party in the October 25, 1993 federal election. Unfortunately, the October 25, 1993 deadline for voting has elapsed, which does take some of the punch out of my endorsement. Perhaps if the Natural Law Party had boiled its campaign platform down to twenty-two pages instead of forty-four, I would have been in a position to endorse its policies sooner.

What most impressed me about the Natural Law Party was that it didn't promise merely to form a good government, or a dynamic government, or an accountable government. The Natural Law Party promised to form a *perfect* government. The leader of the NLP at the time of the 1993 election, Neil Paterson, was also Governor-General of the Age of Enlightenment for North America and a member of the board of directors of Maharishi Heaven on Earth Corporation. I found Mr. Paterson's assessment of his political credentials to be both forthright and optimistic. He said: "I have the scientific knowledge to create a government as efficient as the government of nature."

After more than eight years of Progressive Conservative rule under Brian Mulroney, I sincerely believed the country was ready in

1993 to embrace Heaven on Earth by voting for a party that could deliver a perfect government that operated along the lines of nature. I don't want you to think I'm a sucker for any smooth-talking, transcendental-meditating Governor-General of the Age of Enlightenment. Mr. Paterson and his team had the practical policies to back up their vision. If only more of us had known about them in the autumn of 1993.

The primary issue of the election campaign that year, according to the Natural Law Party, was to determine which political party was competent to create a perfect government. Since the NLP was the only party that had seven thousand full-time Yogic Flyers at its disposal at election time, it understandably felt it had an edge over the other parties. You may have seen one or another of Maharishi Mahesh Yogi's Yogic Flyers in action on television from time to time. Practitioners of this meditation technique sit in the lotus position and move around a room by hopping up and down on their buttocks. This apparently stimulates brain-wave activity to "a point of maximum coherence", while also proving the old adage that we're all sitting on our brains.

Mr. Paterson said the Yogic Flyers were in the process of creating "a strong, indomitable influence of peace and harmony in Canada." This was to be achieved by obeying what the NLP called The Constitution of the Universe. The author of this constitution, according to the NLP, was "a single, self-interacting Unified Field of pure intelligence." (No, not Pierre Trudeau – though the description sounds uncannily accurate.)

On page 31 of the Natural Law Party's 1993 campaign platform, John Hagelin, PhD., described the Constitution of the Universe. I want to quote this description at some length, because I think it's the kind of message ordinary Canadians have been waiting to hear for a long, long time:

The next stage in the sequential elaboration of the self-interacting dynamics of the Unified Field is found in the free-fermionic formulation of the string of four dimensions (L(4)). In this more expressed formalism, all bosonic degrees of freedom associated with the original, abstract space-time arena are fermionized except the two right-moving and two left-moving coordinates needed to account for the four-dimensional structure of classical space-time geometry.

As you can see, Dr. Hagelin was able to predict with great precision the fate of the Progressive Conservative party in the 1993 federal election. Kim Campbell and her troops were indeed "fermionized" except for "two right-moving coordinates" who managed to escape the fury of the electoral mob.

The NLP's concept of perfect government is based on a natural law the party calls the "principle of least action". At first glance, this principle may sound like the working philosophy of the Canadian Senate. But the NLP has something much more sophisticated in mind. For example, the party would like to introduce electronic voting in Parliament. With this system in place, proposals would appear on each MP's video monitor, and the MP would simply press a button to indicate Yes, No, or Reconsider, which would send the proposal back to committee for "refinement". The NLP believes electronic voting would eliminate the need for bitter and divisive debates in Parliament. As the party's official platform so movingly puts it: "Seeing our leaders quarrelling and attacking one another is a deep disappointment to our elders, and damages the delicate emotions of our children."

The Natural Law Party has the resources and expertise to grace this country with a perfect government dedicated to bosonic degrees of freedom associated with the original abstract space-time arena. What on earth are we waiting for?

ROYAL JELLY AND OTHER CONDIMENTS

Battered by months of unfavourable press coverage, Prince Charles recently agreed to submit to an extensive interview on British television. The general assumption is that he did this as the first step in a campaign to convince the British people that he is still fit to be king. In the course of the interview, the Prince claimed that he remained faithful to his wife, Princess Diana, right up until their relationship was clearly beyond repair. By the reckoning of some observers, this means his first infidelity must have occurred a few weeks prior to his Grimm's Fairy Tale marriage to Diana in July of 1981.

Rarely in the history of England's hereditary monarchy has an heir to the throne so urgently required the services of a court magician to spruce up his public image. The only comparable royal PR disasters — all of whom ascended to the throne prior to the invention of public relations — are Edward VII, who abdicated in 1936 to marry an American divorcee; George III, who was insane for the last ten years of his reign in the 1820s; Charles I, who was beheaded for treason in 1649; Henry VIII, who beheaded a number of his wives between 1535 and 1545; and King John, who tried and failed to impose a feudal version of the GST on his barons in the thirteenth century.

In all fairness, Prince Charles' personal peccadillos pale in comparison to the misdeeds of some of his royal forebears. Even Charles' now-legendary 1989 telephone utterance to his longtime friend Camilla Parker-Bowles that he would like to live in her trousers seems rather tame when set against past royal indiscretions.

The problem in today's media-drenched, rush-to-judgment environment is that public figures are expected to behave in an exemplary manner — especially a public figure whose official title is Prince of Wales, Earl of Chester, Duke of Cornwall and Rothesay, Earl of Carrick, Baron of Renfrew, Lord of the Isles, and Prince and Great Steward of Scotland. If I had been in Prince Charles' shoes, I would have been tempted at some point in the television interview to peer directly into the lens of the camera and say to the viewing public, "What would you do if you were in my shoes?"

Noblesse oblige, as the old saying goes. With privilege, wealth and influence comes the pressure to behave in a noble, high-minded manner. Confessing adultery on national television, however sincere the confession, simply won't do. An adulterous heir to the throne is one thing; an adulterous heir to the throne who admits he's an adulterous heir to the throne is quite another.

The issue here is one of fitness for kingship. It's a personality test very few of us are forced to undergo in our lifetime. Would-be kings are unable to campaign for the job the way politicians do, by promising tax breaks, arguing for political reforms, shaking hands and kissing babies. Would-be kings can only shake hands, kiss babies, ride in ornate carriages, cruise on ornate yatchs, have ornate weddings and ornate extra-marital affairs.

Centuries ago in many European countries, an inheritance law was enacted to settle the question of fitness for kingship quickly and conclusively. The law, known as primogeniture, entitles the eldest son of the family to all the toys and whatever else might accrue from the departed father. For the British royal family, what the law of primogeniture means is that the line of ascendancy to the throne is settled not by public referendum or psychiatric assessment, but by a roll of the genetic dice: The first royal sperm to fertilize the first royal egg inherits the throne — as long as the fertilized egg is not female.

Some royal-watchers believe Queen Elizabeth's only daughter, Princess Anne, is the best suited of her children to inherit the throne. But under the rules of primogeniture, Anne is now sixth in line, behind Charles, his two sons, and her two other brothers. In horse-racing parlance, Princes Anne is fading fast.

Others in Great Britain and countries where the monarch is still the head of state — Canada, for example — believe the monarchy should be phased out altogether. They say it's a purely ceremonial institution that has outlived its usefulness and has become an embarrassing burden on the public purse.

I'm of an entirely different view. I think it might be refreshing to create an hereditary aristocracy right here in Canada to run our affairs for us. I realize that blue-bloods inherit more than just a coat of arms and a deer park — for example, they are congenitally susceptible to getting carried away in their enthusiasm for a fine claret and the sport of polo. But there's nevertheless something bracing about the notion of entrusting the fate of the nation to the luck of the biological draw. Considering how we've fared in electing governments in recent years, I'd say it's a calculated risk.

NO REST FOR THE JOLLY

Most parents in the Western hemisphere are approached at one time or another by their children and asked the following question: "What does Santa Claus do in the off-season?" Up to now, parents have had to resort to stock answers about Santa cracking the whip with his army of elf sub-contractors as they fill out countless purchase orders for faxing to wholesale toy distributors the world over in preparation for next Christmas. Some parents still employ the outdated stock answer that Santa, the nebulous Mrs. Claus and the elves are busy making toys. Under the terms of the General Agreement on Tariffs and Trade (GATT), of course, Santa and his elves are specifically prohibited from manufacturing their own toys.

But parents have an alternative answer they can give their kids— an answer more in keeping with the businesslike tenor of the times to which their children must slowly become accustomed: In the summer-time, while his sleigh is being overhauled and his reindeer are grazing on the tundra, Santa Claus networks.

In July of 1995, as part of a busy schedule of meetings, conventions, symposiums and colloquiums, Santa Claus attended the thirty-second World Santa Claus Conference. That year's gathering was held in Copenhagen, the capital of Denmark, whose famous red-light district has no official connection to the customary festive ornamentation of the Yule season. In all, one hundred and thirty-two Santas from fifteen countries attended.

The only sour note was struck by Finland's Santa, who boycotted the conference on the grounds that the other one hundred and thirty-two Santas were imposters. He accused these multiple Santas of confusing the world's children, as though the world's children didn't already experience multiple-Santa sightings every season at their local shopping malls. Ironically, the Finnish Santa's concerns were very much on the minds of the other Santas. A conference guest from Malaysia gave a stimulating talk on the topic of "Strength in Numbers: The Usefulness of Multiple Santas in the Emerging Global Economy."

Notwithstanding the Finnish Santa's reluctance, Santa Claus has no choice but to change with the times. One lecture at the Copenhagen conference — "Positioning Santa in the New Free Markets of Russia and China" — deftly addressed the challenges and opportunities for Santa Claus in regions of the world previously closed to him by rigid political ideology. One of the most well-received talks at the conference, delivered by a delegate from New Zealand, was titled "Toward a

Bipolar Santa: The Benefits of a Second HQ in the Southern Hemisphere".

For the first time in the history of World Santa Claus Conferences, elves were accorded equal standing as delegates. This came as a result of an amendment proposed at the previous summer's conference by the delegate from Zimbabwe. This delegate eloquently deplored the discriminatory practice of inviting elves to conduct informal workshops in the evening hours but barring them from the plenary sessions in the mornings and afternoons. The emotional high point of the conference was an address entitled "Elf Esteem", in which an elf likened his new status as a full-fledged special delegate to similar civil-rights triumphs in the sphere of human affairs. The elf ended his stirring speech with a call for a humane review of the elves' long-term collective bargaining agreement.

Of course, all was not strictly business at the conference. Merriment abounded during optional guided tours of Copenhagen's many tourists attractions, including Charlottenborg Palace and Amelienborg Square. Surprisingly, an informal evening tour of the city's red-light district was attended by all one hundred and thirty-two Santas.

Among the most popular features of the 1995 conference were the brainstorming sessions animated by invited consultants. One session, "Santa On-Line: Room for Reindeer on the Information Highway", sparked much fruitful discussion. So did "Body Image and the Importance of Being a Role Model", sponsored by Weight Watchers, and "New Paradigms of Naughty and Nice", conducted by the American Bar Association.

In the final analysis, the one hundred and thirty-two Santas came away from the 1995 World Santa Claus Conference with a renewed sense of purpose, a collective determination to keep the spirit of Christmas alive, and duty-free tobacco and alcohol.

THE COLOUR OF MARGARINE

Not so long ago, one of the most common questions on the lips of visitors to the province of Ontario, regardless of their place or origin, was: "What on earth is wrong with your margarine?"

Ontarians may have grown accustomed over the years to the way Ontario margarine looked. But people from other provinces and countries often reacted with shock and disbelief when confronted with our dayglo yellow margarine for the first time.

"Doesn't everyone's margarine look like this?" the unsophisticated Ontarian would ask the visitor.

"Not on your life," the visitor would snort. "Our margarine looks like butter."

In Ontario, until very recently, it was against the law to make margarine that looked like butter. Consequently, the colour of Ontario margarine was so bright that it could double as night-light in the kitchen if left out on a counter with the lid off. Ontario was the only province in Canada that prohibited butter-coloured margarine. Thus Ontario was the only province in Canada with a bootleg-margarine problem. Not surprisingly, the problem spread.

On a visit to my mother's home in the late 1980s, I was shocked to find her freezer crammed with huge tubs of margarine. When I asked her about it, she lowered her voice and told me it was Quebec margarine, bought in bulk and smuggled across the Ottawa river for distribution in Ontario.

"Take a look at this," my mother whispered as she pried the lid off one of the tubs.

"It looks like butter," I said.

"Doesn't it? It tastes like it, too. But it costs half as much, and it's soft."

"This stuff is illegal in Ontario," I told her. But she just chuckled.

My mother wasn't alone in her disregard for the law. By the late 1980s, it was estimated that the traffic in smuggled butter-coloured margarine accounted for fifteen percent of all margarine sales in the province. It got so bad in those Prohibition years that the provincial government eventually stopped trying to enforce the colour law. One inspector, whose mandate was to see that the province's Oleomargarine Act was scrupulously obeyed, likened the effort to stop the flow of contraband margarine into the province to that of "fighting with one arm tied behind your back."

When my own mother started trafficking in contraband margarine, I knew the problem had become monumental. She, after all, was the person who first taught me the difference between right and wrong, and who used to spend hours kneading artificial colour into margarine back in the early days of margarine, when it was the colour of lard, before it became the colour of dayglo lard. How long would it be before my mother began wilfully ripping the tags off mattresses and carrying more than the allowed number of groceries through the express checkout counter?

Ontario's Oleomargarine Act, as constituted in the 1980s, couldn't have been clearer: "No oleomargarine shall have a tint or shade containing more than one and six-tenths degrees and less than one-half degrees of yellow, or of yellow and red collectively, measured in terms of the Lovibond tintometre scale." The Act further stipulated that "no person shall manufacture, sell, offer for sale, have in his possession for sale or serve in any public eating place any oleomargarine that does not comply with the provisions of this Act."

And yet an estimated fifteen million pounds of illegal butter-coloured margarine were oozing into Ontario each year at the height of the smuggling trade. In makeshift speakeasies from Cornwall to Fort Frances and Cobalt to Sault Ste. Marie, men, women and sometimes even children exchanged tubs of bootleg margarine for cash. Ancillary criminal activity sprouted up around the illicit trade. Hedonistic merchants served toast and sandwiches that contained illegal margarine and sold them at inflated prices to an impressionable populace. In secluded laboratories, out-of-work chemists lured by the prospect of a quick buck worked around the clock to develop ways of transforming the legal dayglo Ontario margarine into a substance that approximated the colour of bootleg margarine. Astonishingly, the Oleomargarine Act seemed to carry no moral weight at all in the province. Ordinary citizens, in staggering numbers, gladly compromised their standing in the community for the thrill of possessing margarine that looked like butter.

At the height of the crisis, a few civic leaders advocated the quashing of the Oleomargarine Act in favour of a simpler law which would insist only that margarine producers clearly identify their product as margarine. But butter lobbyists warned that if Ontario margarine manufacturers were allowed to use colours other than the officially sanctioned one, Ontario consumers would be duped into thinking margarine was actually butter, and widespread culture shock would ensue.

In retrospect, the only way the tide of contraband margarine could have been stemmed is if police forces in every community had been issued a Lovibond tintometre, along with the constitutional authority to enter homes and test private stocks of margarine at any hour of the day or night. But this didn't happen. Instead, in the early days of 1995, under the cover of the post-Christmas doldrums, the Ontario government quietly informed margarine makers that they no longer would be required to use the bright yellow tint in their product.

Were my mother and the thousands of other citizens who practised blatant civil disobedience for all those years responsible for breaking the moral will of the Ontario government? Not exactly. The real culprit in the case was the North American Free Trade Agreement, under which hundreds of tractor-trailer loads of normally-coloured margarine began to stream unchallenged into the province from the United States. Thus another high moral principle was sacrificed to the expediency of knowing on what side one's bread was buttered.

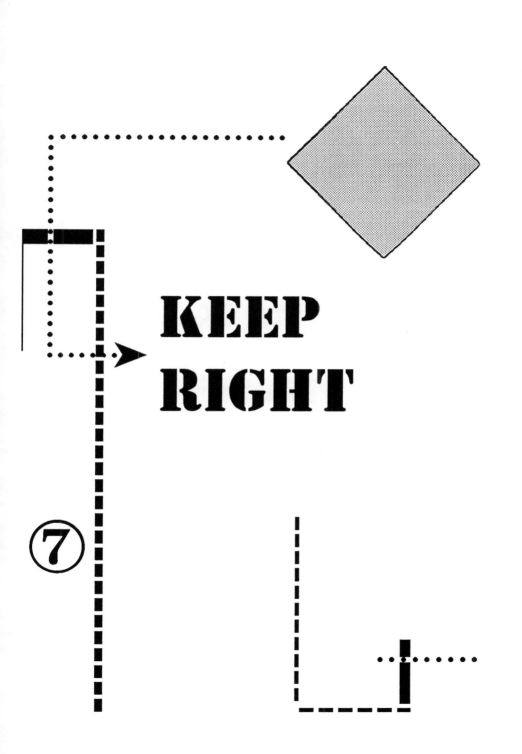

KEEP RIGHT

⑦

A BUM RAP

Magazine stands are suddenly bulging with health and fitness periodicals going by grabby names like *Self* and *Shape*. The philosophy of these publications is that you will probably feel a lot better about your Self if it has a discernable Shape. The magazines offer exercise regimens, detailed graphics showing muscles you never knew you possessed, intricate nutritional advice, ads and articles about swimsuits with flattering and/or forgiving cuts, and inspirational stories about people who managed to get their proliferating buttocks under control.

Being a late arrival to the multi-billion-dollar fitness/wellness craze, I was somewhat intimidated by the muscular definition and general sturdiness of the people whose photographs are featured in these magazines. The fact that the vast majority of the people in the photographs were women only added to my apprehension. After a cursory reading of a few of these magazines, I came to the conclusion that I eat almost nothing that is good for me, that I am physically inactive to the point of indolence, and that I need bi-focals. The magazines have negatively impacted on the shape of my self-esteem.

The reason I acquired a number of these publications in the first place was to become better acquainted with the wellness movement. If I was to have any hope of identifying with the health-obsessed life experiences of the rest of the population, it was important that I know the things they know. For example: "Gone are the days when an apple a day keeps the doctor away," an article in one of the magazines reported. "It now takes half a green pepper, a tomato, ten strawberries, a carrot and a banana." I hadn't realized until I read this article that nutrition was subject to the same inflationary pressures as money. In 1993, the U.S. Department of Agriculture was recommending five to nine servings of fruits and vegetables per day. Heaven knows by how much this amount will have increased by the end of the century.

Another article on nutrition pointed out that many people eat for reasons that have nothing to do with hunger. These reasons may include boredom, depression, elation and anxiety. To combat this tendency, one nutritionist suggested we eat five or six healthful "mini-meals" per day. That way, according to the nutritionist, our body won't have a chance to feel true hunger, therefore we'll know that every one of our cravings is bogus. The upshot of all this nutritional advice, it would seem to me, is that we must now set aside three or four hours per day for the collection, preparation, consumption and avoidance of food we used to wolf down in a matter of minutes.

Abdominal and back muscles are a major concern of the new health magazines. One of them describes a series of "abs" and back muscle exercises as "the foundation on which you'll build your summer-ready body." This doesn't mean the magazines neglect other parts of the anatomy. One magazine recently ran an in-depth feature article, "Seven Great Moves to Boost Your Behind," outlining exercises designed to strengthen the buttocks muscles. The article noted that cyclists and ice skaters tend to have overdeveloped quadriceps, and this overdevelopment often comes at the expense of buttocks muscles. By working the buttocks muscles, interspersing these exercises with at least three weekly aerobics sessions, and eating five to nine servings of fruits and vegetables in the course of five or six daily "mini-meals", one's body could well be "summer-ready" by the summer.

I have to confess I was startled by the amount of space the health magazines devoted to buttocks-related topics. In fact, these topics are also in vogue in the mainstream magazines. I recently spotted a full-page ad in *Cosmopolitan* magazine for a series of workout videos entitled "Buns of Steel." The ad more or less promised that women who purchased the videos and adhered to the fitness program demonstrated in it would be in a position to transform the texture of their rear end into that of processed iron ore.

My surprise at this ad unfolded in two stages. First came my surprise at the use of the word "buns" to denote a woman's posterior. In this sensitive period of inter-gender relations, it would never occur to me to refer to a woman's backside as "buns". (For that matter, it would never occur to me to refer to a woman's backside in any context.) The second stage of my surprise was perhaps more a question of semantics than anything else, but I believe it also touches on a contemporary psychological problem known as a "poor body image". Put as simply as possible: How can buns possibly be made of steel?

Since the use of the word in reference to human buttocks was inspired by its more traditional usage in the world of baking, surely a degree of softness in human buns is not only desirable but essential. In the baking world, buns that had the texture of steel would be deemed unworthy of sale and thrown out as garbage. To the extent that a person's rear end resembles the buns bakers manufacture -- which involves a not entirely savory stretch of the imagination at the best of times -- the notion of transforming a woman's buttocks into steel defies esthetic common sense and probably contributes to the inaccurate and self-deflating body image of many women.

An alternative colloquial term for the human posterior — "butt"— has come into vogue in recent years. If anything, this term is even more indelicate than "buns". Three primary definitions of the word "butt" in my Oxford dictionary are: "object of ridicule", "thicker end of a tool or weapon", and "mound behind a target". People who read *Cosmopolitan* aren't likely to want their rear end thought of in any of these contexts.

There is a potential two-pronged solution to this problem:

1. The makers of the "Buns of Steel" video should change the title to reflect a more realistic transformation of women's behinds -- Buns of Polyethylene, for example. Polyethylene is a tough, light plastic that denotes both durability and flexibility.

2. A more anatomically correct term from the world of baking, such as "kaiser rolls", should be selected to represent the rear end. "Kaiser rolls" imply freshness and pliability, but also a robust, imperial quality.

Kaiser Rolls of Polyethylene: There's a fitness goal we would all be proud to achieve.

ADD WATER AND STIR

A shocking thing has begun to occur at house parties, in the workplace, during sporting events and wherever else men gather for business or pleasure: They're exchanging recipes.

I know this for a fact because I have done it myself a number of times. I have been on the receiving end of recipes from other men and I have given recipes of my own to them. A few weeks ago I even dictated a Caesar salad recipe to my aunt, who grew up in an age when men ate their food without passing comment and would never have dreamed of preparing a meal, let alone doing so from a written script.

Most recently, I received a recipe for raisin bran muffins from a man with whom I regularly play golf. The previous week, he had brought a few of his muffins to the golf course, and we ate a couple of them prior to the round.

"Am I tasting brown sugar?" I asked him.

"Molasses," he said with a smile.

"Interesting," I said.

"I can give you the recipe."

The latter statement carried a slightly unsettling whiff of taboo, as though we were socially and perhaps genetically programmed not to exchange recipes, and so derived a perverse thrill from doing so.

"I'd like that," I said.

The next week, as we took our golf clubs from the trunk of the car, the man unfolded a piece of paper and handed it to me. "The muffins," he said by way of explanation.

"Fine," I said, folding the sheet of paper and stuffing it quickly into my pocket.

"That's my only copy, so could you make a duplicate?"

"No problem," I said. "I'll photocopy it after our round."

He nodded and we made our way to the first tee.

There is no law on the books anywhere in the world, with the possible exception of certain inordinately macho Latin American countries, that specifically forbids men from transcribing and exchanging recipes. But something about the ritual tends to undermine the gruff, action-oriented role we were trained for in childhood. (Of course, you could argue that now that Clint Eastwood has directed and starred in *The Bridges of Madison County*, nothing traditionally masculine is sacred anymore.) Many women I know have surrendered the recipe-exchanging role without a fight. At social gatherings, you'll often see knots of women talking earnestly about workplace issues while the men discuss the relative merits of semi-sweet chocolate, or the correct way to grill squid on the barbecue.

Men have yet to reach the intuitive stage of cooking. Most of us practise this art with devout concentration, not unlike a child who has recently begun to walk. One Saturday evening this past spring, my brother and I spent several hours leafing studiously through my mother's voluminous collection of recipes. She sat and watched us, pleased that we were enjoying ourselves, yet slightly unnerved by the spectacle of grown men spending a Saturday night scrutinizing the components of Apple Brown Betty.

"Lately," I told one male friend, "I've developed an interest in the visual appeal of food as opposed to merely how it tastes."

"I know what you mean," he said. "Diced red pepper, for example."

"Exactly," I said. "Presentation counts for a lot."

"You bet," he said.

A year or two ago, we might have been discussing Mike Tyson, or how the designated-hitter rule upsets the delicate strategic balance of baseball.

My first experimentation with the use of a wider colour palette in my cooking occurred many years ago, when I thought it might be fun to augment Irish-style mashed potatoes — potatoes and chopped green onions — with small wedges of tomato. My multi-coloured mashed potatoes were an instant hit. Only my future wife, who for some arcane reason believed in the strict segregation of potatoes and tomatoes, was less than thrilled. What was important was that I was setting the scene for my eventual development into the kind of man who would exchange food-preparation ideas with other men without fear of ridicule or of forgetting where I filed the recipe, which is what happens nine times out of ten.

Does the fact that they exchange recipes make men more gentle, sensitive, nurturing, attentive, thoughtful and environmentally friendly? Probably not. Changes in social and genetic imprinting take a long time to occur. Rome wasn't built in a day. Even something as simple as an overnight salad isn't ready until the next morning.

THE SINGING DENTIST

I was in the waiting room of my dentist's office, nervously reading a six-month-old newsmagazine about a war in a distant republic, when the noise of an industrial-strength drill — more a jackhammer than a drill — rattled the walls. I had noticed some workers in the hall on my way in that morning. Surely one of them, and not my dentist, was operating the drill. Renovations were being done throughout that floor of the building, so a certain amount of industrial-strength drilling was probably unavoidable. But why here? Why now?

In recent months, through great diligence and because the condition of my teeth left me no choice, I had made considerable progress in the battle to overcome my fear of dentistry. I no longer dreaded a visit to the dentist for weeks prior to the actual appointment. I no longer spent hours dreaming up elaborate excuses to stave off appointments at the last minute, such as the one about being abducted by aliens who physically examined me and also cleaned my teeth, which I had tried out on my dentist the previous year. I no longer drenched my clothes in sweat whenever I was finally cornered in the Chair. But the sound of the drill in the hall was starting to undermine these hard-won gains.

"It's just like the way you feel about mice," I explained to my wife earlier that morning, when she tried to downplay my fear of dentistry.

"Mice are different," she said.

"Yes: They're small, they're afraid of humans, and they can't hold any instruments."

"I have an actual phobia about mice," my wife said. "They carry disease. Dentists prevent disease."

"I am deathly afraid of disease prevention," I said, which effectively put an end to the conversation.

I tried to concentrate on the newsmagazine. The war in the distant republic was going badly. I wondered: Do people in war-torn parts of the world get to postpone their dental appointments until hostilities cease? Then a fresh-faced young hygienist appeared in the doorway and smilingly said something I couldn't make out over the din of the drill. The drill fell silent for a moment and the hygienist said: "We're ready to do you."

My dentist is an affable man who likes to sing along with the music on the radio as he works. Such is the extent of my dependence on his moods that as long as he sings, I relax. As soon as he stops singing, whether it's to switch from one gleaming, pointy instrument to another or to mumble an instruction to the hovering hygienist with the hose, I stop relaxing. In the world of natural science, this kind of relationship is known as symbiosis. In the world of psychology, this kind of relationship is known as pathological.

"That wasn't your drill I was hearing in the waiting room, was it?" I asked the dentist with a nervous chuckle.

"What?" he said sharply.

"The noise of a drill. That wasn't —"

"Three days I've been listening to that thing," he said. "They haven't even finished the work on the air ducts. How the hell am I supposed to practise in these conditions?"

The dentist's question must have been rhetorical, because he was deploying a tray of gleaming, pointy instruments to the immediate left of the Chair. I had never seen him in such a bitter mood. I was about to ask him if he would rather re-schedule the appointment when the sound of the drill in the hall resumed. By the time the sound stopped again, a number of the dentist's instruments were inside my mouth.

Soon the smell of burnt enamel wafted up my nostrils as the dentist's drill, pitched high as a dog-whistle compared to the din from the hall, excavated a tooth. My only hope, as always, was that the anesthetic would kick in by the time the drill struck paydirt. The fact that the dentist wasn't singing, and that I couldn't even hear the radio, didn't help matters.

"How are we doing?" the dentist asked with a friendly pat on the knotted muscles of my shoulders.

"Huhee-ohee," I replied, which was a garbled version of "hunky-dorey", which was a specific lie I told only when I was in the Chair.

Occasionally, to console myself while in the Chair, I meditate upon the experience of St. Apollonia. She was the member of a prominent third-century family of Alexandria who infuriated her father by converting to Christianity. Her father obviously had big-time pagan ambitions for Apollonia, because he was so enraged by her conversion that he personally reported her to the authorities, who were conducting a full-scale persecution of Christians at the time. On February 9, 250, Apollonia was tied to a column, her teeth were extracted one by one without the benefit of anesthetic, then she was burned alive. Apollonia's symbols in Christian art are pincers and a tooth. Toothache sufferers and dental phobics can pray to her for intercession. This is what I began to do that morning. My prayer was quite simple: "Please, St. Apollonia, make my dentist sing."

A quarter-hour into the session, a burly man clad in khaki trousers and a khaki shirt and khaki socks and shoes sauntered into the room carrying a khaki metal toolbox. At first I thought he was an hallucination brought on by the second injection of Novocaine I had requested and received from the dentist.

"It's about bloody time," the dentist muttered to the burly man.

"Don't blame me," said the man. "Work needed to be done on the floor under you before I could do anything here."

"Then why did you tell me you'd be here yesterday? Open wider."

I opened wider and waited to hear the burly man's explanation.

"Look," he said, "it's not like yours is the only plumbing system in the building."

"I'm not saying that," the dentist replied, emphasizing key words with the drill. "All I'm saying is that it was you —"

"Umf," I grunted in pain.

"— who told me —"

"Ummf."

"— that you would do the work yesterday."

"Uummmf!"

My dentist looked down at me. "How are we doing?"

"Ree ring," I said.

"Say again?"

"Ree. Ring."

The dentist removed his drill and hand from my mouth. "I can't make out what the hell you're saying."

"Please sing," I said, blinking rapidly.

"Sing?" said the dentist.

I blinked imploringly.

The dentist chuckled. "I never realized anyone could actually hear me."

"I love it when you sing."

"Maybe he's not in the mood to sing," the plumber said as he bent down to open his toolbox.

"Who asked you?" I snapped at him. By now my entire central nervous system was tingling from the Novocaine.

"Easy now," said the dentist. "Let's all try to get along. Open wide. . ."

In the corner of my eye I watched the plumber take a monkey wrench in hand and wriggle under the sink not three feet from where I sat supine, defenceless and open-mouthed. Instead of singing, the dentist began to have a conciliatory chat with the plumber while they both worked. Together they were exploring their loose bond of workmanship, whereas I was alone in my victimhood, and the smiling hygienist didn't seem to be entirely of this world.

"People always hate having to call a plumber," the plumber mused from under the sink. "But dentists have the worst image of all. Nobody likes a dentist."

That's not true, I wanted to say. Many people admire dentists enormously.

"That's because of Hollywood," the dentist said as he put a new bit on the end of his drill. "You see all kinds of movies where the hero is a doctor, but how many movies have you ever seen with dentists in them?"

"*Little Shop of Horrors?*" the otherwise mute hygienist suggested with a smile. The hygienist thus broke one of my cardinal rules, which was: Never Tease A Dentist.

"Or *Marathon Man,*" the plumber grunted from under the sink.

Marathon Man: The ultimate taboo topic for dental phobics: Laurence Olivier as a crazed dentist who tortures Dustin Hoffman with a drill. The plumber, whose hairy, half-exposed buttocks provided the only visual relief in the otherwise gleaming, pointy room, had blithely uttered the title of that appalling movie while I reclined in the very shadow of a dentist and his instruments and the various grievances he had carried into this morning.

"You ever see *Marathon Man*?" my dentist asked me.

I shook my head so violently that it dislodged his index finger from the back corner of my mouth.

"No?"

"Umf," I said, even though there was nothing in my mouth. The last thing I wanted was to say or do anything that might further contaminate his state of mind.

"Olivier overdid it," the dentist said. "These drills have enough torque of their own to do the work. Olivier handled the drill like it was a jackhammer, as though he had to press real hard to penetrate the enamel of Dustin Hoffman's teeth." Then he glanced down at me and said, "How are we doing?"

I grunted hypocritically, wholeheartedly, hoping my enthusiasm would finally inspire him to sing along with the radio none of us could hear.

The plumber slid out from under the sink and said, "I can't imagine a drill that small would have much torque. I've got drills five times that size that are pretty sluggish."

"Come here and give it a try," the dentist said. He looked at me. "You don't mind, do you?"

The receptionist called me at home an hour later to apologize on behalf of the dentist and explain that it was all a joke, that the dentist had never seriously intended to let the plumber try out the drill on me.

"Could you hold a moment?" the receptionist said. "He'd like to speak to you directly."

The next thing I heard on the line was the dentist, his voice thin and faint, singing a few bars from a Phil Collins tune I happened to detest.

BACKWARD CAPS: THREAT OR MENACE?

Several years ago, when boys and young men began to wear baseball caps with the brim pointlessly jutting out from the back of their head, I thought it was a passing fad, like multi-coloured Mohawk haircuts and safety pins through the nostrils. But while Mohawk cuts and safety-pinned noses have all but vanished, backward baseball caps have become more common, if anything. Nowadays, even men in their late twenties wear their baseball cap backward, as though doing so somehow keeps them in touch with their adolescence, which no one in their right mind should keep in touch with for longer than is absolutely necessary.

When I was young, the only person who wore a baseball cap backward was a baseball catcher. He wore his cap that way for the perfectly good reason that the brim didn't fit inside the mask he was forced to wear to protect his head. The general consensus in those days was that catchers looked like idiots for this reason.

Yet now, despite the fact that a baseball cap worn backward is as idiotic-looking as it was in the past, boys and young men seem psychologically bound to continue wearing them that way. They are apparently trapped in a cycle of mild delinquency in which any potential decision to turn the brim of the cap to the front of the head would be viewed as an unacceptable concession to people like me, who hate the sight of backward baseball caps.

With the recent release of an in-depth report from the Montreal Neurological Institute on the long-term health hazards of wearing a baseball cap backward, young people from all walks of life now have a compelling reason to change their mind. The study, supervised by renowned neurosurgeon William Beresford-Howe, monitored the brain activity of more than one hundred young men who had been wearing their baseball cap backward for a year or longer and found an alarmingly consistent pattern of neurological irregularities.

Dr. Beresford Howe explained that the strap of a baseball cap presses harmlessly against the hard occipital bone at the back of the skull when the cap is worn as it was designed to be worn. But when the cap is worn backward, the strap impinges on the less well-protected frontal lobes of the brain in the upper forehead area, eventually triggering a variety of serious brain disorders. Said Dr. Beresford-Howe: "The first step we must take, from a preventive standpoint, is to strongly urge all young men to immediately stop wearing baseball caps backward. If young men fail to implement this advice, governments must be prepared to enact appropriate legislation to force the baseball-cap industry to stop manufacturing these potentially lethal items."

The litany of ailments Dr. Beresford-Howe and his team of researchers uncovered in their examination of chronic backward baseball cap-wearers is appallingly long: impaired short-term memory, decreased reading skills, apathy, aggressiveness, myopia, inner-ear disorders, skin cancer, blackouts, impotence, sterility, partial paralysis and premature senility.

"In many cases, these symptoms are fully reversible over a period of time if the patient immediately stops wearing his baseball cap backward," Dr. Beresford-Howe said. "But beyond a certain point, the pressure of the cap strap on that part of the skull begins to have a permanent effect on nerve impulses in the highly sensitive frontal lobes. To put it bluntly, young men who wear baseball caps backward are unwittingly and slowly performing a frontal lobotomy on themselves."

This stunning conclusion goes a long way toward explaining the often worrisome academic testing results that have come out of our high schools and post-secondary institutions in recent years. Instead of blaming teachers, the curriculum and budget cuts, responsibility can finally be placed where it belongs—on baseball caps worn backward.

All citizens have a role to play in confronting this public-health crisis. If you have a loved one, friend or acquaintance who wears a baseball cap backward, please pass the findings of Dr. Beresford-Howe's study on to them. Copies of the report will soon be available in regional health unit offices.

With a combination of vigilance by the general public and a comprehensive information campaign, the scourge of backward baseball caps can and will be eradicated. Dr. Beresford-Howe's goal is to take all non-essential baseball caps out of circulation by next April Fool's Day. Let's make that our goal, too.

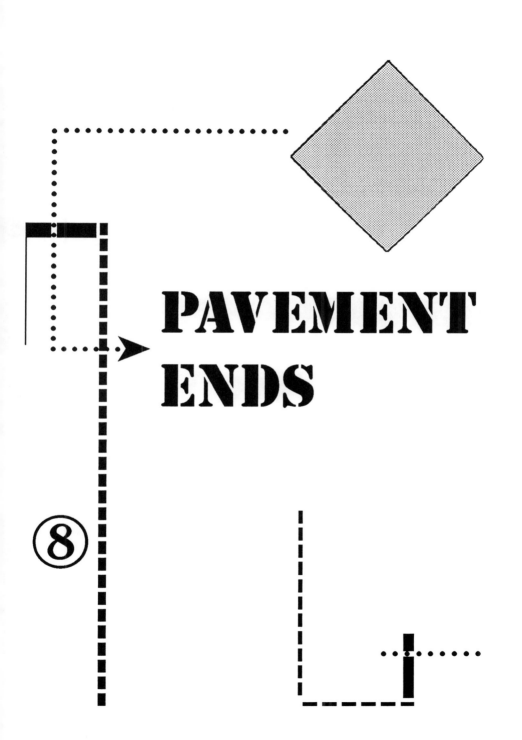

PAVEMENT
ENDS

⑧

THE DISENCHANTED FOREST

The general principle by which I guide my actions while hiking in the wilderness is that I'm never as safe as I think I am, and I'm never in as much danger as I think I am. In other words, I have absolutely no idea what is going on out there.

Ages ago, when the mastodon and the wildcat ruled the woods, people didn't have the spare time to wander through it for recreational purposes. Back then, individuals who walked in the wilderness fell into one of two distinct camps: They were searching for food or they were about to become food. Occasionally the two camps overlapped, but those who were searching for food were generally alert enough to flee predators before the predators fled them. This is why human beings evolved into technologically sophisticated creatures, whereas today's wild animals are as technologically primitive as yesterday's wild animals.

Walking through a dense forest is not at all like walking through a dense urban area. The forest is much, much safer. Nevertheless, most forest paths feature periodic arrows or swatches of paint on tree trunks to guide hikers through the woods. Some paths also contain "points of interest" at which plaques with maps, diagrams and accompanying texts explain to you why you are having such a good time. Regardless of what the plaques indicate, a substantial number of unpleasant things have happened to people in the forest in the folk tales of various cultures of the world. The aptly-named brothers Grimm, who parlayed their cruel hobby of compiling stories that frightened children into a lucrative career, set many of their grimmest tales in the forest. Hansel and Gretel got into a major situation there. The Big Bad Wolf stalked Little Red Riding Hood there. Assorted unsavoury fairies, imps, gremlins, elves, satyrs and other musky-smelling creatures made the forest their year-round home. Ask a child if she knows a story involving a forest and she will almost invariably tell you of something horrid that happened to someone.

Well-designed boots can solve some problems, but the age-old mystical enchantment of the forest is something against which even the most up-to-date backwoods outfitter is hard-pressed to recommend equipment. No less an authority on enchantment than Merlin,

King Arthur's trusty wizard, wound up eternally imprisoned in an oak tree after revealing the secrets of his magical knowledge to someone by the innocuous name of Vivien. This is what can happen to you in the bush.

Once, as a young man, in the merry month of May, I ventured into the woods with some friends to do a bit of brook-fishing. There had been a light frost overnight, but the temperature rose quickly in the morning. The quality of light through the half-grown foliage was enchanting.

At that age, I had no idea that enchantment wasn't a desirable state of mind in the forest. I was so callow and idealistic that I thought enchantment was an end in itself. So did an awful lot of people who grew up in the 1960s. We courted enchantment wherever we went, in the mistaken belief that it would make us at one with the universe. In those days, we tended to think of the universe as a benign and charming place to spend our life. A state of enchantment seemed the ideal way to savour the fruits of this Eden into which we had been born. Sometimes, when I had nothing to do on a Friday night, I would compose odes to this enchanting universe. Here's one of them:

> *O universe of endless enchantment,*
> *I can't find the words to describe you.*

My ode was brief but to the point.

Feeling Byronic and suffused with the nameless glee of perpetual youth, my friends and I blazed a trail that bright May morning to the babbling brook where, with any luck, we would terminate the lives of a handful of unsuspecting speckled trout.

As the temperature rose and the morning breeze dwindled, I noticed that my friend Richard, who was at the head of our hiking party, had begun to wave his arms in a frantic manner. At first I thought Richard was symbolically clearing the cobwebs from the previous evening's over-enthusiastic indulgence in the enchantment of Molson's Export Ale.

"Hey Richard," I cried with youthful good cheer, "stop making like such a geek."

Richard half-turned to answer me but was instead overcome by an even more frantic urge to wave his arms. That was when I began to notice undulating pointillist clouds hovering above and around us.

"Blackflies," said the other Richard in our group, who was the most seasoned woodsman.

Richard — the less seasoned one — turned toward us. The white of his eyes were those of a spooked horse. By now he had thrown his fishing rod aside and was hopping as well as waving, in joyless mimicry of a brief dance craze inspired by a mediocre rock 'n' roll rock group of the '60s called Freddie and the Dreamers.

"He's about to freak out," the more seasoned Richard observed.

"It seems to me he's already freaked out," said a third Richard who, in terms of woodsman seasoning, was midway between the other two Richards but evidently had a more acute understanding of the limits of human nature.

"We'll have to get him out of here," said the most seasoned Richard.

"What— and not go fishing?" I said.

"It's something about my skin, some chemical in it," the least seasoned Richard sobbed from the head of the line. Then, without warning, he burst from the rude trail into the bush itself, screaming and gesticulating as he went.

"Somebody go after him," said the second most seasoned Richard.

"Are you crazy?" said the most seasoned Richard. "The flies are worse in there. That's why moose and bear wander onto the highway. After a while they can't stand the flies any better than Richard can. It's known as *Dementia rusticosis*. Richard will have to hit rock-bottom somewhere in there, go into a kind of Carlos Castaneda trance state, locate his astral body, escape into it, then guide his physical body back out to the highway to flag down a car."

"What if he doesn't know how to go into a Carlos Castaneda trance?" the other Richard asked.

"Then he will die," said the other-other Richard, which effectively bummed us all out, which was a state of consciousness diametrically opposed to enchantment, which was why we were in the woods in the first place.

Richard scowled at our shiny, dejected faces. "Where is it written that nature is supposed to be fun?" he asked us. "Do you think the little trout in the brook like being slaughtered? Do you think the young foxes and minks and wolverines enjoy watching their parents die slowly in leg-hold traps? Do you think the little plants don't mind being trampled by us on our way to the brook, and that the brook doesn't mind it when we go for a leak in it?"

"Richard," I said, "you're bumming us out. There aren't any wolverines in this bush, are there?"

"That's the least of your worries," Richard said with a look of triumphant contempt in his eyes. I decided at that moment I didn't like or trust seasoned woodsmen. There was something feral about them. Only the approaching wail of an undoubtedly rabid fur-bearing animal enabled me to break free from his demonic glare. The approaching wail turned out to be the least seasoned Richard, who had miraculously strayed back onto the trail despite the fact that his T-shirt was pulled over his head. His shoulders and chest were speckled with tiny black bugs that were feasting on his blood.

"I'm going home as soon as we catch some fish," he said in a high, thin, delirious voice. "Point me to the fish. Somebody, please. I just need a couple of fish. . ."

"I'll take you to the car," I muttered, making an about-face and pushing him roughly back in the direction of the highway.

That night, I tried to convert our adventure into a suitable poem, but all I could come up with was:

> *O indifferent universe of bottomless pain,*
> *I never want to be at one with you again.*

Every environment has its hierarchy, and the forest is no exception. Elite hikers, clothed from head to foot in expensive water-retardant clothing, carrying everything they need for an extended stay in the bush in a pack on their back, are for obvious reasons knows as backpackers. These people possess two easily identifiable characteristics:

1. A pack on their back.
2. A chip on their shoulder toward more casual woodspersons.

My wife and I once encountered a couple of overnight backpackers at a secluded lakeside campsite that happened to be on a trail that was also popular with day-use hikers such as ourselves. It was mid-morning, a lovely plume of blue smoke was curling up from the fire over which they had undoubtedly prepared a breakfast of sunflower seeds and petrified apricots. Now that their breakfast was mercifully over, the two backpackers where doing what backpackers did between hiking and eating grotesque food substitutes, which was to sit in a kind of daze by the embers of the fire.

"Howdy!" I called out to them as we approached. They looked up, briefly, then resumed staring glumly at the remains of the fire. "Peach of a day," I added. "The fish will be biting like crazy, assuming you're so inclined."

It's a fact of human nature that, in the presence of an unduly laconic person, one is inclined to restore the balance of communication by blathering on about whatever comes to mind. I realized this was happening to me with the two taciturn backpackers when I found myself holding forth on Giambattista Vico's theory of the cyclical nature of history and the ways in which it diverged from the Cartesian world-view.

"You have to bear in mind," I said to them as my wife tugged on my sleeve and implored me under her breath to come away, "that Descartes thought of the world as a machine, entirely divorced from the mind, and that it was only through the intervention of God that the mind could experience the world. Vico, on the other hand, asserted..."

My voice trailed off as the male backpacker rose from his semi-lotus position by the fire, brandished the stick with which he had been poking the embers and said, "Why don't you go take a hike."

I was shocked by this flagrant breach of woodland etiquette and told him so.

"Scram!" he said, taking two sidelong steps toward me with the stick held high, like the apeman with the bone in his hand at the beginning of *2001: A Space Odyssey.*

This is when I realized that I was in the midst of a defining woodland moment – a situation designed to test my ability to adapt to the harsh realities of life in the wild. "Who's gonna make me?" I asked the backpacker.

"Me and this stick," the backpacker replied.

Desmond Morris has written often and well on the territorial impulse in animals. Obviously this particular backpacker had "gone native" at some point during his sojourn in the woods and genuinely believed this patch of land was his to defend against all interlopers. I, on the other hand, carried civilization in my metaphorical backpack. I loved trees and lakes and squirrels and mythical beasts as much as the next person, but I could not turn my back entirely on the rich legacy of the Enlightenment – things like parallel parking and the Dewey Decimal System. I thought of Descartes, who said all human emotions were rooted in the body, and that by controlling the physical expression of emotions you could control the emotions themselves. I knew Descartes was out to lunch on that point, but I nevertheless decided to put his theory into practice.

"Well, have a great day," I said to the backpacker, nodded with a smile at his moribund companion and turned tail to catch up with my much wiser wife.

The moral of this story is: Unless you yourself are a serious backpacker, give them as wide a berth as you would any woodland creature.

ALL THE NUDES THAT'S FIT TO PRINT

A friend who is a ski enthusiast clipped an advertisement he spotted in a newspaper and passed it along to me. The ad was for a family nudist resort. It extolled the virtues of all the healthy activities a person could enjoy at a nudist resort: ". . .swim, jacuzzi, workout, sauna, tan, play tennis, ping-pong and pool, cross-country ski, jog, fish. . ."

Cross-country ski?

The prospect of gliding through the hinterland on a well-groomed trail under a placid blue sky on a crisp winter's day – without any clothes on — seemed less than invigorating. Only later did it occur to me that nudists probably wore toques and boots when they went skiing. I suppose the majority of us are fairly naive about the logistics of this particular lifestyle.

I was first exposed to nudism the way most boys were, by furtively leafing through a nudist magazine. A tobacco store not far from where I grew up carried a few of these magazines. They contained photographs of people playing volleyball, having picnics and generally doing the things groups of families and friends did on a fine day, except they had no clothes on while they did them. I don't know if stores still stock nudist magazines, but at one time I suppose they responded to a demand in the hobbyist market the same way model-railroad or true-confession magazines did.

My interest in nudism back then had little to do with the quest for a viable hobby or lifestyle. My interest was mainly anatomical, spurred on in equal parts by curiosity and hormonal imperatives. Sometimes, while the proprietor of the tobacco store went looking for an obscure brand of pipe tobacco for one of his adult customers, I would grab a magazine from the rack and rifle through it. Invariably I came away humbled and pensive, my boyish imagination agog at the prospect of playing volleyball bare-naked with my grandparents.

My next contact with nudism occurred while watching television in the living room of my very own home. This was back in the days of the Doukhobour protests. The Doukhobours were a Russian religious sect whose members lived mainly in southern British Columbia in the 1960s. Their main claim to fame among the general Canadian populace was that certain radical elements within the sect were inclined to protest government policies by setting fire to buildings and taking all their clothes off. The CBC television news footage that was welded to my memory one evening in the '60s was of a group of Doukhobour ladies standing naked with their backs to the camera in front of a burning building. These ladies were certainly not candidates for pictorials in any of the men's magazines that were starting to appear at that time. For one thing, the ladies' thighs had dimples, which Hugh Hefner and the other skin-mag magnates were dead-set against. I believe even the most egalitarian nudist magazine might have turned these ladies down.

Being an impressionable youngster, the experience of staring at the naked bodies of large, mature ladies while in the presence of my mother and my grandfather and my older brothers demonstrated to me that entirely new vistas of personal embarrassment were out there, waiting to be stumbled into. I believe my mother tried to defuse the situation by saying something to the effect of: "Look at that building burn."

Much later, in the autumn of 1980, I spent a few days in the French Riviera, where most women don't bother to wear the tops of their swimsuits. This struck me at the time as an eminently sensible approach to swimming and sunbathing – not that I was asked my opinion. By this point in my life I was a mature adult, so nudity was no longer the terrible and fascinating thing it had been to me when I was a boy. Now it was merely fascinating.

I was nevertheless taken aback by what I witnessed on the shores of the Mediterranean Sea. Each morning, the dirty old men of the town of Nice would gather at one end of the promenade overlooking the pebble beach and spend the next few hours sauntering up and down it. The men openly ogled the bare-breasted females on the beach, and actually paused every now and then to applaud one of them.

From what limited knowledge I have of nudist resorts, its members have long since evolved past the point of ogling one another. (Otherwise, how could they play a proper game of ping-pong?) In family nudist resorts, where naked bodies are commonplace, there's nothing titillating or even especially interesting about them. Nudists seem to have conquered the age-old obsession with naked skin. I think this is admirable and I take my hat off to them. Just my hat.

AN ECLIPSE OF THE ECLIPSE

We chose Hamilton's splendid Royal Botanical Gardens as the location from which not to watch the solar eclipse of May 10, 1994. After paying a nominal fee of $8.50 to enter the arboretum, we wandered the grounds awhile in search of the ideal vantage point for not watching the sun be obstructed by the moon while eating a cappacola sandwich. (We were the ones with the sandwiches, not the sun.)

We finally settled near a grove of magnolia trees in fragrant bloom. Part of the reason we chose this spot was because the Canada geese who made the arboretum their year-round home seemed not to have colonized it yet. The main evidence of this was the absence of copious goose stools on the ground.

Prior to leaving the house, I had fashioned a primitive pinhole camera from two pieces of white cardboard. The pinhole camera, through a complex optical process I won't go into here and now, produces an exact image of the sun, though smaller than lifesize, on one of the two white pieces of cardboard. Apparently this was one of the few safe ways to view a solar eclipse. At first I felt a bit sheepish standing in the arboretum with my back to the sun, looking down at two pieces of cardboard. But when the tiny black disc of the moon began to pass in front of the tiny white disc of the sun on one of my pieces of cardboard, I felt better.

While my wife poured us coffee from a thermos, a man of fairly advanced age wandered over and asked me why I was staring at cardboard. I told him to step closer and adjusted the angle of the cardboard to get the sharpest possible picture of the cosmic conjunction. The man leaned close to me, peered at the faint projected image and said nothing for a long time. All I could hear was our breathing.

"How does it work?" he finally said.

"I'm not an astronomer or anything," I said, "but apparently the relative positions of the earth, moon and sun line up at certain times and because of —"

"I don't mean the eclipse," the man said irritably. "I mean what I'm seeing here, the little fuzzy picture of it on the cardboard."

"It's a pinhole camera," I said.

"This is a camera?" the man said.

"It doesn't take permanent pictures or anything, but it works like a camera."

"Explain."

"Well, the hole I made in the cardboard with a pin functions as the lens, and then. . ."

"Then what," the man said.

"Well, the rays of the sun get focused as they go through the pinhole, so that the —"

"How do they get focused," the man demanded.

". . . They just do."

"Like magic?" said the man.

"In a way," I said defensively.

"And you won't show me how the trick works."

"Listen, sir, the eclipse will soon be at its peak, so if you don't mind I'd like to —"

"You don't know, do you? You don't know anything about how your own camera works."

"It's not 'my' camera," I said. "It's just two pieces of cardboard. Anybody could make one."

"Right," the man said over his shoulder as he walked away. "But you're the only boy-genius in the arboretum who did, because you don't have the guts to take a peek right at the sun."

I watched the man vanish around a clump of pine trees, then I turned to my wife and said, "Is he crazy or something?"

My wife shrugged.

"Guts have nothing to do with it," I said. "Doesn't he know we're not allowed to look directly at an eclipse?"

Although shaken by the man's derision, I concentrated on lining up the pieces of the cardboard for the moment when the eclipse became annular — that is, when a ring of sunfire would be visible around the full disc of the obstructing moon. Various media reports had indicated that a pinhole camera was one of the best ways to watch this phenomenon without destroying one's retinas. Apparently welder's glass was another. But the media coverage of the eclipse prior to the event had concentrated so intensively on the physical hazards of looking at the eclipse that I feared welder's glass might only be safe for people with welder's eyes.

As the moon progressed across the face of the sun and the sky and surrounding parkland eerily darkened by a few notches, a rush of alarm suddenly coursed down my spine like an electric current: I realized we had left our cat at home without instructions of any kind on how to defend herself against the eclipse.

"Our bedroom window faces south," I said to my wife. "What if she jumps up on the sill, noses her way through the blinds and stares at the eclipse?"

"Why would she do that?"

"I don't know. For the same reason humans do. Cats are even more curious than we are. They're always staring at something."

"She'll be fine," my wife said.

I was unconvinced. As the birds in the arboretum switched to their evening program of music, I pictured our cat hearing the same songs at home, wondering why they were being sung in the middle of the afternoon, walking into our bedroom, jumping onto the sill, nosing her way through the blinds and staring at length at the eclipse.

It was one-twenty in the afternoon and the sky was a strange, dim shade of blue. My heart was rattling in my rib cage. I felt the way certain sensitive animals did just prior to an earthquake. "We've got to go home," I told my wife.

"Why?" she said.

"Isn't it obvious to you by now? So I can blindfold the cat!"

"Look," my wife said, pointing.

We watched in awe as a ring of sunfire around the black moon became visible next to the coffee stain I had accidentally made on the little piece of cardboard.

"Incredible," I said. "Now let's go home."

For the rest of my life I will remember the dim, spectral light inside our house that afternoon. The moon had not finished crossing the path of the sun when we arrived home. The shadow of our neighbour's maple tree was an exquisite filigree on the pavement of the street.

It was clear to me from the eerie expression on our cat's face that she had been seriously affected by the solar eclipse. "You didn't stare at the big, bright fire in the sky, did you?" I asked her. "You didn't look at the black circle that came in front of the big, bright fire?"

The cat said nothing and merely went on looking zonked. Then she wandered off to the kitchen and half-heartedly pounced on something imaginary at the foot of the oven.

The next total solar eclipse in central Canada will be on April 8, 2024. Somewhere on earth, at least two total eclipses are visible every year. Like Lot on the outskirts of Sodom, we must always be prepared to look away.

CANADA DAY ON THE BEACH

I was so mellow by the end of a languid Canada Day on the beach at Port Dover that I barely blinked when a forty-five kilogram weakling kicked sand in my face.

It had been a classic afternoon for relaxing in the sand. A mild offshore breeze nudged unthreatening clouds out over Lake Erie, the air temperature was moderate, the take-out perch stands were doing brisk business and the beach itself was a crazy-quilt of semi-clothed human beings in various states of repose.

The first thing I thought as I lay down and closed my eyes was that the sound of a high summer day on the beach hadn't changed a bit since I was a boy. Little children still shrieked excitedly in the bathwater-warm shallows; rock 'n' roll music still played on portable radios; the same scent of aromatic lotions and unguents wafted on the breeze, and parents called out to their wandering children in the same frantic, totally unself-conscious tones. Only the cut of the swimsuits changed, and not always for the better.

Young men and women who felt they possessed physiques worth parading still did so on the smooth, cool sand at water's edge. Babies in bonnets lolled obliviously in the shade of an umbrella. A man of a certain age fell asleep on his voluminous stomach. A younger man made a grandiose swan-dive in three feet of water to catch an errant frisbee. A large extended family spread out an enormous blanket right next to us, immediately switched on a radio tuned to a country music station, then vanished en masse into the water.

Despite the din, I drifted into a pleasant daze that Canada Day afternoon, the sunlight glowing red through my closed eyelids. I always brought a book with me to the beach but I rarely read more than a few paragraphs. The bright light, distant horizon and great vault of sky did the work of a general anesthetic. You probably could have performed open-heart surgery on me as I lay there, beached, half-consciously celebrating the birth of the country.

Rather than sleep, I meditated lazily upon the fact that Canada Day was probably the blandest imaginable name for our national holiday. Since Confederation, political leaders had bestowed no less than five different official names on the day. Originally, the holiday to commemorate the creation of Canada was known as The First of July. After prolonged and agonizing debate, the name was officially changed to July The First. In retrospect some people felt this was a rather trivial alteration. Then came those who felt the name of the July 1 holiday should reflect the nature of the event the July 1 holiday was intended to commemorate. So the name Confederation Day was officially adopted. But some people still felt the name didn't adequately capture the distinct nature of Canada. So the name was changed yet again, to Dominion Day.

Our country was officially christened the "Dominion of Canada" in 1867, in honour of Psalm 72. The psalm states, among other things, "He shall have dominion also from sea to sea, and from the river unto the ends of the earth," which amounts to an uncanny description of the geography of Canada. Under the Constitution Act of 1982, "Dominion of Canada" is still the official title of our country. But for reasons that have never been clearly explained, the generic term Canada Day was chosen by our legislators to replace Dominion Day in the early 1980s. It became the fifth and probably not final name of our national holiday.

The proximity of our national holiday to that of the U.S. on July 4, combined with the Canadian government's habit of changing the name and its former policy of floating the holiday on the first Monday in July, may have contributed to confusion among some Canadians as to what exactly they were celebrating, and when, and what it was called, and why it was called that. While Canadians tried to sort out all these variables, Americans simply gazed up at the red glare of their rockets on July 4 and said, "Oooooooh!"

This, I decided that afternoon on the beach at Port Dover, was the essential difference between the two countries. There was something forever provisional about Canadians' notion of Canada, as though it were a fine summer day that couldn't possibly last forever. Our perennial identity crisis was symbolized by the constantly changing name of our national holiday. No wonder we celebrated it rather passively and tentatively, by doing the things we would most like to do on a precious summer day, such as sharing a stretch of beach with loved ones and a crowd of fellow citizens.

The forty-five kilogram weakling who jolted me out of my patriotic reverie by kicking sand in my face wasn't challenging me to a fight or making any personal or political statement. In fact, it's probably unfair to call him a weakling, and potentially inaccurate to say he weighed forty-five kilograms. The facts are as follows: He was a boy, he was with a friend, and the two of them were performing a full-tilt giant slalom through a beachful of prone bodies to the water. One of the boys tried to make a sharp turn near where I was lying and kicked up some sand that landed on my face and in my open mouth.

My first instinct was to sit up and berate the child. But he was long-gone. My wife helpfully suggested that if I didn't sleep with my mouth open I wouldn't have got sand in it.

"I wasn't sleeping," I said, "I was thinking about our country."

"That doesn't explain why your mouth was open," she said.

I'm not entirely sure she was right about that.

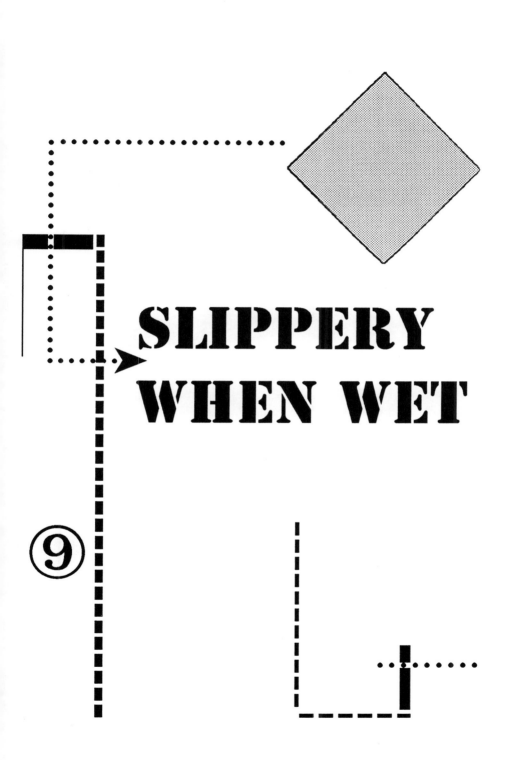

SLIPPERY WHEN WET

⑨

IS THERE A SPIN DOCTOR IN THE HOUSE?

*Truth never comes into the world but like a bastard, to the
ignominy of him that brought her forth.*
— Milton

Legend has it that the father of the American republic, George
Washington, didn't tell a single lie in his lifetime. If this legend is
accurate, the fact that Washington managed to have a brilliant political
career despite this potentially devastating handicap is one of the more
inspiring stories in all the annals of history.

As far as I know, not one Canadian leader, going as far back as
Samuel de Champlain and the Jesuit missionaries of New France, ever
boasted of not telling a single lie. Trade with the native North Americans and the prospect of exporting a fortune in minerals and other
resources to the Old World were predicated to a considerable degree
on whoppers. Even back in those days of primitive advertising and
marketing techniques, the truth wasn't exactly prized as being instru-
mental to the amassing of personal and national wealth. Then as now,
nothing greased the wheels of commerce quite like a shrewdly bent
fact. The incoming Europeans routinely misrepresented their long-
term plans in the New World to the various people of Asiatic descent
who had arrived there first. The natives, for their part, hoodwinked the
early French explorers into believing there was a kingdom full of
fabulous riches up the Saguenay River, when in fact there were only
more rivers, lakes, muskeg, fur-bearing rodents and blackflies. Whether
we like it or not, lies of all kinds are woven into the political and
economic tapestry of human life.

Despite this long tradition, the word "lie" still carries a strong
whiff of opprobrium. So nowadays in political circles, words like
"spin" and "gloss" are used to describe the time-honoured art of
telling the truth selectively. And even though the conscious manipula-
tion of facts for political purposes has been going on since time
immemorial, there's still room for innovative minds to pioneer new
contortions. Consider the landmark case of Shelly Martel, a cabinet
minister in the former Ontario government of Bob Rae. In 1992, Ms
Martel became the first person in the history of civilization to take a lie

detector test to prove that she was telling the truth about having told a lie.

When the test results showed that Ms Martel had indeed told the truth about having lied, her notion of personal and political propriety crossed over into an ethical twilight zone in which perhaps only Rod Serling could have accurately explained to us what sin it was that she was not guilty of committing.

Ms Martel took the lie detector test in the hope of clarifying the circumstances behind a cocktail party in Thunder Bay in December, 1991 at which Ms Martel, during a heated argument, said that a Sudbury doctor was facing criminal charges in connection with his health insurance billings. The Sudbury doctor in question was naturally distressed by these remarks, especially since they came from a provincial cabinet minister, and Ms Martel subsequently confessed that she was lying when she made them. Instead of resigning from the cabinet, Ms Martel decided the best way to clear her name would be for her to pay to undergo a lie detector test to prove that she had indeed lied about the Sudbury doctor. Her implicit rationale was that telling a lie was a lesser crime than peering into a confidential medical file and blurting some of its contents at a cocktail party in Thunder Bay.

One can well imagine how a transcript of the 1992 lie detector test might read:

TEST OPERATOR: What is your name?

MARTEL: Shelly Martel.

OPERATOR: What is your present occupation?

MARTEL: Minister of Northern Development.

OPERATOR: Were you lying when you said you were telling the truth about the Sudbury doctor in December of 1991?

MARTEL: Yes.

OPERATOR: Are you lying now?

MARTEL: About what?

OPERATOR: About having lied about telling the truth?

MARTEL: No. I'm telling the truth about having lied about telling the truth.

OPERATOR: Were you telling the truth when you implied it was a lie that you were lying about telling the truth?

MARTEL: No. The lie I told was about the truth I didn't lie about when I wasn't lying about telling the truth.

OPERATOR: Is that the truth?

MARTEL: So help me God. I couldn't possibly tell a lie about something that wasn't true, unless the lie I was telling was different from what wasn't the truth to begin with, which certainly wasn't the case in this case.

OPERATOR: Can you hold on a moment, Ms Martel? The machine seems to be overheating or something. . .

The most serious potential drawback of any career in public life is that politicians can't afford to keep their mouth shut. It was George Washington who said, "I hold to the maxim, no less applicable to public than to private affairs, that honesty is the best policy." But it's worth remembering that in Washington's day, not everything a politician said and did was subject to blanket coverage by news reporters and subsequent dissection by pundits with any number of axes to grind. Prior to the advent of twenty-four hour news channels, television cameras in legislative chambers and *People* magazine, a politician's character was more a question of public faith than of verifiable fact. In view of this, it might have been too easy to rush to judgment against the embattled Ms Martel, even if we found her notions of rectitude somewhat convoluted.

Who among us hasn't been tempted at one time or another to rent the services of a lie detector to help get us out of a jam? Who among us hasn't employed bafflegab or some other diversionary tactic to bend the facts in our favour and stave off personal or professional disaster? Who among us doesn't wish we were capable of conceiving such a confusing justification of our actions that people would simply give up trying to make sense of us, as happened in the Martel case?

If anything, Ms Martel's bizarre lie detector defence was a valuable reminder that in public life, a coin has as many sides as you can get it to stand on.

THE NEXT IDENTITY CRISIS

Prior to the technological revolution of the twentieth century, personal identification was a simple concept: You had a name, which you probably didn't know how to write.

Generations ago, when the tax collector or anyone else in an official capacity asked you what your name was, you simply told it to them. If the official doubted this was your real name, a neighbouring peasant would be called in to attest to your honesty.

"His name is indeed Theobald, your excellency," the neighbour would attest.

"And what is his last name?" the official would demand.

The neighbour would ponder this for a long time, then declare: "His last name is also Theobald, your worship."

"This man's full name is Theobald Theobald?" the official would inquire sceptically.

"That's correct, your magnificence," the neighbour would reply and hastily leave.

When the official asked you to write your name, you told the official you preferred it if he wrote your name on your behalf. When the official misspelled your name, you didn't realize it, since you could neither read nor write. Besides, Theobald Theobald wasn't your real name. Your real name was Richard, Son Of The Blacksmith With Bad Breath.

And so your twentieth-century descendants inherited your misspelled name, which eventually was embossed on any number of sophisticated plastic cards with which your descendants are able to purchase consumer goods they can't afford, receive health care they can't afford, place long-distance phone calls they can't afford, and many other important twentieth-century conveniences.

The descendants of some of your craftier fellow peasants currently make a living manufacturing counterfeit personal identification. They sell these documents to people who are not satisfied with the various rights and privileges accorded them under their actual name. This is another innovation of twentieth-century technology, and it has forced governments and corporations to ponder more foolproof ways of accurately identifying their fellow citizens.

In Ontario, where photo radar surveillance on the highways was recently abolished by the government of Premier Mike Harris because it was considered an unwarranted intrusion on the privacy of bad drivers, politicians are considering a plan which would involve the fingerprinting of all citizens. Under this plan, one's fingerprint would appear on a new identity cards alongside, I would expect, one's name, photograph and social insurance number, with room in the bottom corner for one's DNA profile when it becomes economically feasible to draw a blood sample from all of us.

The convenience of a fingerprint, as opposed to the name Theobald, is that a fingerprint is thought to be unique to each person, in the same way that no two snowflakes are exactly alike and no two automobiles have exactly the same system for flipping the front seat forward. Early in this century, fingerprinting replaced the Bertillon system of measuring the skeleton and other body parts as the best way to identify and keep track of criminals. (The old system was named in honour of Alphonse Bertillon, a nineteenth-century French criminologist and skeleton-measurer.) Fingerprinting still plays a major role in criminal investigations, and we should probably have foreseen that it would eventually be considered as a way of monitoring the entire populace. All too often, government agencies presume the citizens they serve are guilty until proven too lazy and unambitious to commit a crime against the state.

We have been registered, photographed, numbered, catalogued and cross-referenced as much as any generation of human beings in history. A line has to be drawn somewhere, and we should draw it on our hands. We should tell our government that we would rather disfigure our fingers by dipping them in hydrochloric acid than submit to compulsory fingerprinting. (Then again, perhaps an industrial-strength bleach would do the trick. I think hydrochloric acid would dissolve our fingers altogether, which might be an unnecessary overreaction on our part.)

Before they came to power, Ontario's Conservatives advocated the development of a "smart" identity card containing a computer chip with personal information encoded on it. The Conservatives felt that such a card would foil counterfeiters and provide enough space for all the information governments at all levels need to know about us. Both compulsory fingerprinting and "smart" ID cards are fundamentally un-Conservative notions. Mr. Harris should re-think these ideas immediately as part of his ongoing common sense revolution. I'm not suggesting Mr. Harris should think instead about a simple cardboard card with the name THEOBALD THEOBALD handwritten on it. I'm sensible enough to realize we can't all be called Theobald Theobald.

THE GREAT DEBATE

The federal election of 1993 radically altered the political map of Canada. The Liberal party returned to power for the first time in almost a decade, the separatist Bloc Quebecois formed Her Majesty's Loyal Opposition, the Western-based Reform Party thwarted any chance the outgoing Progressive Conservatives might have had of forming a bridge foursome, let alone a viable political force, and the federal NDP faded into even deeper obscurity than usual.

The results of the 1993 election also fundamentally changed the nature of political discourse in Canada, perhaps forever. For those citizens who came of age at a time when the country's political agenda was more easily discernable, a perplexing time had begun.

So with more than a little nostalgia, I take you back to a memorable debate that occurred during the federal election campaign of 1988, when Brian Mulroney was seeking a second term in office and the issues were so much simpler. The three party leaders who participated in this debate – Mr. Mulroney, John Turner and Ed Broadbent – have all since moved on to other pursuits. But who in Canada can forget the spirited, substantive exchanges that occurred that evening on an issue of paramount importance to the nation?

Here are a few highlights.

BRIAN MULRONEY: Let me begin by asserting that our government is on the record as fully supporting the principle of a free and unfettered climate, subject of course to Quebec's historic veto over this matter, in keeping with that province's customary right to limited self-determination within the purview of a strong, united Confederation, from sea to shining sea, come rain or come shine.

ED BROADBENT: This is just another example of a Conservative government abdicating its constitutional duty to administer the climate equitably from coast to coast. Are we to have a two-tiered climate in this country: one climate for the poorer and remote regions of Canada, and another climate for the wealthy business interests in central Canada who traditionally support the Conservative Party?

JOHN TURNER: If I may interject here —

MULRONEY: There goes Mr. Broadbent again, perpetually forecasting overcast skies and low-pressure systems. It's my government's stated belief — in fact, we regard it as a sacred trust — that the various regions of this country have the necessary wisdom and resources to manage their own climate, within the limits of their constitutional jurisdiction. It is not our government's intention to dictate the weather to the whole country, as a New Democratic Party government would undoubtedly wish to do.

BROADBENT: And what of regional disparities, Prime Minister? For example, how does your government intend to compensate the people of Yellowknife, who shovel snow from September to late May, compared to the people of Victoria, who can sit back and watch the crocuses come up in February? Does your government not believe in a fair and equitable climate for all Canadians, regardless of where they live?

TURNER: If I may get a word in edgewise —

MULRONEY: Certainly we believe in a fair climate for all Canadians. But we also hold the conviction — in fact, we regard it as a sacred trust — that, to a reasonable degree, wherever possible, natural barometric forces should dictate the climate. Your party, Mr. Broadbent, would no doubt wish to set up costly and cumbersome weather offices at the border, and to impose punitive tariffs and other counter-incentives to a climate of free trade between nations. Probably you would wish to regulate every aspect of the climate, enacting an unwieldy system of equalization factors that would result in the same weather from coast to coast. This is what the Liberals tried and failed to do for years under Mr. Trudeau. I don't believe it's good for Canada and I don't believe it's good for Canadians. Furthermore, I don't believe it's good for the country or for the people who live in it. Perhaps Mr. Turner would care to enlighten us by commenting on his Liberal

predecessor's disastrous National Weather Program and other inter-
ventionist policies that drove foreign meteorologists out of our country. Perhaps Mr. Turner would like to tell us why he timidly acquiesced
to the Trudeau tradition of handing out plum weather-office jobs and
other Environment Canada appointments across the country to Liberal
party hacks and bagmen, rather than to the most qualified available
people.

TURNER: As you well know with regard to those appointments, I
had no option.

MULRONEY: Oh yes you did, sir. You could have said no.

BROADBENT: Or, or. . . you could have said maybe and in the
meantime established a task force to examine the practice with a
mandate to make sweeping recommendations within a two-year period.

MULRONEY: Or you could have called a snap election on the
issue.

BROADBENT: Or you could have held a first ministers' conference at Meech Lake to search for a broad national consensus on the
right climate for our times.

MULRONEY: Or you could have put the question to a free vote in
Parliament, as our government so honourably has done on one or two
occasions.

TURNER: I suppose I —

MULRONEY: Or you could have said yes but meant no, as our
government so honourably —

TURNER: I think we've strayed from the topic of this evening's
debate, which is the Tory government's dismal record on managing
Canada's climate.

MULRONEY: You could have said no, Mr. Turner, but you did
not.

TURNER: All right. I could have said no.

MULRONEY: Mr. Moderator, if I may be allowed to say something
in all honesty.

MODERATOR: All right, but just this once.

MULRONEY: Thank you for your indulgence, Mr. Moderator. I
just to want to say that I will not rest until this government has fully
achieved its goal — in fact, we regard it as a sacred trust — of fostering a

climate in which all Canadians, regardless of where they came from or where they live, can look to a bright and sunny future.

BROADBENT: Under your leadership, Prime Minister, the only way Canadians can look to a bright and sunny future is by emigrating to Grand Cayman Island.

TURNER: I wish I had said that.

THIS BEER IS YOUR BEER

What makes Canadians tick? It's a question that endlessly baffles Canadians and endlessly bores the rest of the world.

The rest of the world seems to feel we are a rather tedious nation — a sprawling community of would-be Americans who don't have the necessary self-confidence to be loud and uninformed when travelling abroad, as genuine Americans are. To the British, whose quiet desperation we try our best to emulate, Canadians are would-be Australians who don't have the necessary lack of breeding to be exuberant on their native soil, as genuine Australians are. To Australians, many of whom are descended from eighteenth-century pickpockets and consequently enjoy travelling discreetly abroad, Canadians are a pleasant people who don't have the guts to play rugby without a jock strap.

But how do Canadians feel about themselves? What is our true self-image beyond the cliché that we lack pizzazz and tend not to wear out heart on our sleeve, or sometimes even in our rib-cage?

I always think of Fred Davis, the long-time host of CBC television's *Front Page Challenge*, when I think of the archetypal Canadian. (For that matter, I always think of *Front Page Challenge* when I think of the archetypal Canadian television program.) Canadians will tolerate flamboyant individuality for only so long, after which they turn to Fred Davis for solace. This is perhaps why, in an international survey in the late 1980s, Canada was seen as the second most boring country in the world, after Singapore. But the real truth about the Canadian psyche is that it surpasses all understanding. By and large, Canadians are even more inscrutable than people from the Orient were once reputed to be. In fact, we're so inscrutable that we can't properly scrute ourselves.

For years, I have taken the unscientific but nevertheless instructive approach of using television beer commercials as a barometer of our national self-esteem. Beer, after all, is a substance that Canadians consume in world-class quantities. The manner in which this national pastime is depicted on television can perhaps provide us with some much-needed insight into ourselves.

In the infancy of television commercials, Canadian beer producers spent most of their time and money devising ways to promote their product without actually showing it. In those prohibitive days, even the sight of an untouched stubby brown bottle of beer was considered beyond the pale. The result of this broadcasting regulation was the first spate of "lifestyle" beer commercials. The lifestyle most frequently depicted in these early commercials was that of persons apparently on the verge of consuming beer, though the actual substance was never in evidence.

But by the early 1970s, after the international public-relations triumphs of Expo and Trudeaumania, Canadian beer commercials began to reflect a looser, more confident approach to ourselves and our way of life. Viewers began to see actual beer being poured into actual glasses on TV ads – though no one was allowed to take a sip. Then, in the overheated economic climate of the 1980s, "lifestyle" beer ads came back into vogue with a vengeance. Instead of endless depictions of blue hot-air balloons and untouched glasses of beer, viewers began to see fun-loving young Canadians having wild beer-sodden parties in the city and at the lake. Ironically, we still didn't see anyone actually having a beer at any of these parties.

In the pinched economic climate of the '90s, brewers have had to work hard to sustain a level of beer consumption that once came naturally to Canadians. Nowadays, new variations on beer, and marketing gimmicks to rekindle our love affair with the beverage, come and go with alarming frequency. A marketing gimmick of particular sociological interest surfaced in 1993, when a product called "ice beer" was the focus of an intensive ad campaign.

These ads, so different from all the beer ads that came before, pointed to a new and possibly deeper national malaise. Two competing brands of ice beer employed two separate long-haired, sinister-looking men in overcoats as their advertising spokesman. Each of these men made their sales pitch against a sombre, somewhat Frankensteinian backdrop. Neither of the men would have been remotely at ease at a beer-sodden party in Muskoka, or even at a more sedate function in the city. These were quintessential loners who perhaps had done time in prison. Meanwhile, for reasons known only to the advertising community, a third brand of ice beer adopted a marketing campaign that lampooned the nerdy scientific optimism of the '50s. These ads told us nothing intelligible about the product, and left us with the faint suspicion that our past was somehow bogus and laughable.

As a potential consumer of beer, I was as uncomfortable with the long-haired, pock-marked sociopaths in dark overcoats as I was with the dweeby pseudo-scientist. Judging from these ads, the Canadian beer industry was in the throes of a self-destructive phase. Could this have been a subliminal response to a nihilistic Canadian self-image that came into vogue at some point during Brian Mulroney's nine years as Prime Minister? Had endless rounds of unproductive constitutional squabbling broken our national spirit and robbed even beer-drinking of its primeval appeal? Had Canadians given up all hope of feeling good about themselves and their beer?

I was prepared to draw that sad conclusion when two significant developments occurred in 1995: Several brewers simultaneously devised a new product called "copper beer" with which to entice a dispirited buying public, and one of the major brands built an excessively noisy ad campaign around the most assertive, self-justifying slogan in the history of Canadian beer commercials: I AM.

There may yet be hope for the future of what's left of this country.

ECONOMICS 101 (REMEDIAL)

When I was a boy studying mathematics in school, I wondered what all those tedious hours could possibly add up to in the grand scheme of things. I recognized the need for a solid grounding in the fundamental operations of math — namely, adding, subtracting, multiplying and dividing. I understood that if I went to the corner store and bought a Popsicle without a proper understanding of these operations, I could be cheated out of my rightful change by an unscrupulous and more mathematically adept merchant. It was only after I had mastered the fundamental operations and was then expected to learn more esoteric aspects of math such as algebra, calculus and trigonometry that I began to balk.

I was aware from an early age that it would not be in my best interests to pursue a career in any of the hard sciences. So I sincerely doubted any purpose was being served by daily mental wrestling matches with integers, irrational numbers and other mystical manifestations of high math. Surely my time could have been better spent learning how to repair a toaster. But I was informed by a succession of math teachers and guidance counsellors that my knowledge of mathematics would indeed help me to repair a toaster, and to perform a multitude of other useful tasks, as well. The true purpose of studying math, I was told again and again, was to develop the mental discipline to solve practical problems in all areas of life. I was promised that a good grounding in math would, for example, help me better understand on a personal and collective level the basic mechanics of a national economy.

With all due respect to the pedagogues of the land, that promise was never kept. I understand the mechanics of national economy about as well today as I did in grade one, when I was asked to subtract a one-digit number from another and, in lieu of doing so, burst into tears. I refuse to carry the entire burden of guilt for my present ignorance of how an economy works. In fact, I blame the people who run the economy as much as myself. Their economic policies are an enigma wrapped in a mystery inside a wet blanket.

Take inflation. For years and years, Canadians endured the exhortations of one finance minister after another that they must work together to wrestle inflation to the ground. Inflation, we were informed again and again in the 1970s and '80s, was Public Enemy Number One. If we could somehow get it under control — the preferred method in those days was to moderate our wage demands at work and to tolerate high interest rates at the bank — then surely the rest of the economy would kick into gear and prosperity would be within the grasp of all Canadians, including Newfoundlanders.

In my young adulthood, when the spectre of "double-digit infla-tion" hung over the land like one of the plagues of Egypt, I enjoyed listening to the stories of older people who got their start in the working world in the '50s and early '60s. These were people who had a three per cent mortgage on a house they bought for a couple of thousand dollars and was now worth half a million. I was given to understand that the key to the phenomenal growth and economic stability of that period was the fact that inflation was under control. When wage and price controls and other unpopular measures were introduced in the 1970s, it was based on the view that inflation was the fly in the economic ointment. Some Americans believed at the time that inflation was actually a Communist conspiracy, though subse-quent events demonstrated that the Communists were incapable of organizing a closet, let alone a global economic war.

Cooler heads explained to us that inflation was actually the key symptom of an "overheated" economy, which was a lot like an over-heated automobile in terms of one's ability to make it up a steep hill. In an overheated economy, the delicate balance between production and consumption had been disrupted, and punitive fiscal policies such as high interest rates were necessary to cool consumers off and restore an acceptable temperature to the economy.

More recently, the focus has been on "protecting" the Canadian dollar on the international currency markets, as though the Canadian dollar were incapable of protecting itself. The favourite tactic to pro-tect the dollar has been to raise interest rates. In fact, high interest rates seem to be viewed by our economic policy-makers as being useful in fighting everything short of a yeast infection.

So in the late '80s and early '90s, the Bank of Canada rate was kept high to ward off inflation and to protect the Canadian dollar from foreign bullies. And by the summer of 1992, thanks to these vigilant efforts on our behalf, the national inflation rate stood at its lowest point in thirty long years – 1.1 per cent. Yet unemployment was obscenely high and the Canadian economy was in a coma, as though it had been wrestled to the ground along with inflation.

What went wrong?

One of the problems with contemporary economics, as with contemporary art, is that we always need someone more qualified to decipher it for us. On a person-to-person level, economic matters can be extremely straightforward:

1. I borrowed some money from you.
2. You wanted the money back some time ago.
3. I haven't paid you yet.
4. You're threatening to break my legs.

But once economic activity attains a certain level of complexity — for example, when I borrow money from a third party in order to pay you back before you break my legs — the simple formulas no longer pertain. The trend in recent years has been toward ever more abstract substitutes for money and all the activity money entails. As a result, economic notions have become even more thickly shrouded in jargon, euphemisms and paradigms. A priesthood of economic consultants, advisers and gurus has sprung up to interpret it all for us, but they're as hard to decipher as the information they're supposedly deciphering.

The people in the federal finance department, the Treasury Board and the Bank of Canada may truthfully understand what they've been doing to the Canadian economy in the past couple of decades. But I certainly hope they don't presume anyone else out there understands. To someone with only an average grasp of the subject, recent Canadian economic policy looks like a case of someone tinkering at length with a toaster and somehow turning it into a defective radio.

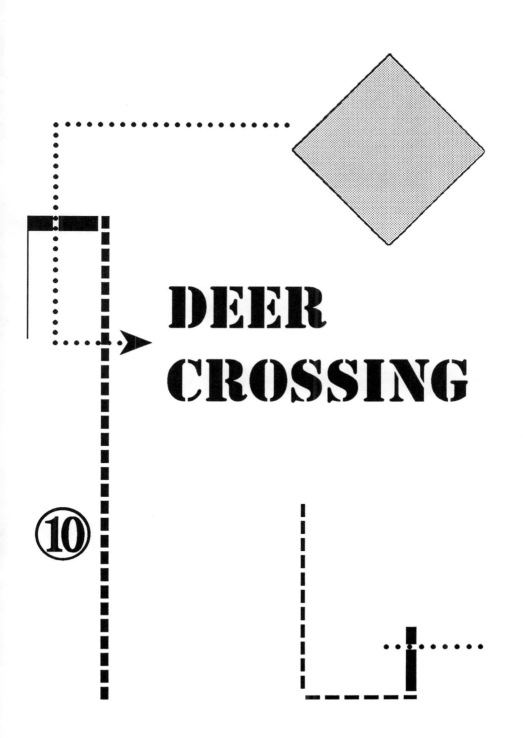

DEER CROSSING

⑩

RODENT PERSONALITIES

1

Every spring, the soil of my backyard is littered with peanuts in shallow graves. The peanuts have been buried in no discernable order, which is probably why the squirrels who hid them the previous autumn have long since forgotten where. I assume squirrels are the culprits because I know of no other animal species that goes to the trouble of burying peanuts. For that matter, I know of no other animal species that begs peanuts from human beings.

I acquired my rudimentary knowledge of squirrel behaviour from years of watching my mother feed the ones that came to her backyard again and again for handouts. A few summers back, the feeding frenzy was at its peak. My mother had what looked like a fifty-kilogram sack of peanuts in a small closet near her back door. The squirrels arrived in her yard with the regularity of air traffic at Pearson airport.

"How many of them do you suppose you're feeding?" I asked my mother one day as we watched a large black squirrel negotiate her narrow porch railing and stuff two peanuts into its surprisingly roomy mouth.

"I don't know," she shrugged.

"What if it's always the same squirrel that comes back every ninety seconds for more peanuts?"

My mother dismissed the idea. "No squirrel could possibly eat that many peanuts."

"What if it stores them somewhere?" I said. "Isn't that what squirrels are famous for? Isn't that where the term 'squirreling away' comes from?"

"Shh," said my mother. "Here comes Blackie."

Blackie, in point of fact, was indistinguishable from all the other hyperactive black squirrels who came to my mother's backyard to beg for peanuts. But through some arcane process of identification, my mother had taken a shining to one of the squirrels, christened it Blackie, and favoured it by feeding it peanuts right out of her hand.

"How do you know Blackie is Blackie, and not any old squirrel?" I asked her as the squirrel alleged to be Blackie gingerly approached her open hand.

"I just know," she said.

The habitat of Blackie and its cohort has grown considerably in the past couple of decades. The only squirrels I ever saw when I was growing up in Northern Ontario were red squirrels that were only slightly larger than chipmunks. It was on a visit to Toronto in the late 1960s that I first spotted the larger, rat-like grey and black squirrels that lived in the parks and ravines of that city. These squirrels exuded urban sophistication and ennui as they scuttled from parkbench to parkbench, stopping only to clutch and eat the discarded corner of a sandwich or some other pittance. The smaller northern squirrels, on the other hand, possessed some of the spirited innocence for which the chipmunk is justly celebrated. But the city squirrels adapted so successfully to their urban habitat that their numbers got out of hand. And so, like the human denizens of Toronto who invaded Huronia, Muskoka and points further north for breathing room and lake frontage, some of the city squirrels migrated. Today, the smaller squirrels that once lived happily in the bosom of many northern communities have been pushed back into the forest by the ruthless scavenging tactics of transplanted city squirrels.

The thing that struck me about Blackie and all its identical relatives is that, apart from their bushy and expressive tail, they were the kind of rodent against which one might be moved to set traps almost as readily as my mother was moved to hand-feed peanuts. I didn't share this observation with my mother, because I realized how fond she was of the squirrels in her backyard. But two developments eventually led to her disenchantment with Blackie and company. For one thing, a number of squirrels found a way into her bird-feeder, along with a dozen or so pigeons who took to wandering in a maddening daze in her backyard when they weren't wrestling with the squirrels for access to the seeds. But the real turning point in my mother's relationship with squirrels in general and Blackie in particular was the day Blackie, in its zeal to get my mother's attention while she was occupied indoors, impaled itself on the screen door of the back porch and hung motionless from it like a ridiculous little pelt.

Because of the unwitting charity of someone who has not yet been disenchanted by squirrels, my backyard is a mass-grave of uneaten peanuts. A squirrel would need the memory of a Macintosh to recall where they're all hidden. The squirrel who did the burying probably remembered the location of only as many peanuts as were needed to get through the winter. The rest of the buried booty amounts to squirrel landfill, the garbage of an over-affluent community of rodents.

A small part of me feels bad for the squirrel, because it's always sad when hard-won wealth is deposited and then forgotten. I did roughly the same thing more than twenty years ago with four dollars and change in a savings account at a branch of the Toronto Dominion bank in downtown North Bay.

Meanwhile, at my mother's, the squirrels are long gone and so are the pigeons. If I'm lucky, I can scare up a handful of cashews in a bowl in her living room at Christmas time, but that's about the extent of her largesse.

2

In the wine-producing world, certain years are known to produce superior vintages. More or less the same rule applies to the world of mice and rats.

I'm not saying that a good wine and a good rat tend to coincide through the years. For all we know, an excellent crop of disease-carrying rodents may turn up in a year in which the quality of the wine is indifferent, at best. What I am saying is that certain natural conditions, such as the weather and the amount of decaying garbage lying around, can have a direct bearing on the respective hardiness of the grape crop and the rodent population. While the verdict was not yet in on how 1993 wines stacked up against previous years' offerings, the official word had already come down from those in the know that 1993 was a very, very good year for mice and rats.

The reasons for the rodent boom of '93 are still open to conjecture. Some experts believe mice and rats experience periodic surges in fertility, in which their already appalling reproductive abilities are further enhanced. Consider the common house mouse, so named because it likes to live in your house: The female of this species produces a litter of four to eight mice after a gestation period of only three weeks. When conditions are right, the house mouse can breed year-round. This means it can be pregnant with eight mice as many as seventeen times in one year. On a good year— which 1993 apparently was —a single house mouse could give birth to one hundred and thirty-six mice. Further compounding the problem is the fact that baby mice are capable of giving birth to baby mice of their own by the time they're two months old. This is why there's always a certain urgency to capturing and/or killing a mouse as soon as possible after it infiltrates your house. I would need a slide rule to calculate it accurately, but I estimate that the mouse population in a single house, if left un-checked, could grow from zero to more than thirty-five thousand in the course of a single year.

The mouse that lived in the cupboard of our kitchen for several weeks at the height of the rodent boom of '93 was highly intelligent, promiscuous and omnivorous —the Madonna of the mouse world, if you will. It lived for food, sex, bowel movements and a warm place to sleep. I tried out several popular brands of mousetrap on it, but this mouse had the instincts of a cat burglar and the nerves of a neurosurgeon. Over the course of several weeks, it liberated a broad range of food products—cheese, chocolate, peanut butter, red jujubes —from various mousetraps without once triggering the sophisticated spring-driven mechanism that was designed to whack the daylights out of it.

I began to sense I wasn't dealing with an average mouse the evening I set out a new trap painstakingly covered with peanut butter at the exact point on the trap where the slightest jiggle would set it off. I checked the trap less than fifteen minutes after deploying it and discovered that it had been picked perfectly clean. Instead of its executioner, it seemed I had become this mouse's special friend — someone who regularly left out treats to encourage it to take up permanent residence in our cupboard, be fruitful and multiply exponentially, as mice are wont to do. By the time I got around to baiting the trap with a red jujube on the advice of a neighbour who seemed to know what she was talking about, the mouse was spoiled rotten. For several days it turned its snout up at my paltry offering and waited for something more palatable.

My wife is passionately afraid of mice. Her fear somewhat complicated our kitchen routine during the great rodent boom of '93. In order to avoid having to open any cupboard doors and possibly cause the sudden exit of a highly motivated and overfed mouse, we stopped storing anything in the cupboard. Everything sat out on the counter or on the floor. Conversely, my wife decreed that everything still inside the cupboard was strictly off-limits until the mouse was dealt with, at which point it would all be thrown out. The news I tried hard to keep from her was that by this point, the mouse had been living long enough in our home to have given birth to eight more mice.

The final battle of the war, which I put off as long as I could because I thought it was unsportsmanlike, involved the use of bio-chemical weapons in the guise of food. Mouse poison, which slowly dehydrates a mouse to death, struck me as the coward's way out of the problem. I vastly preferred the idea of a quick kill in a trap, followed by a proper Christian burial in a Glad bag surrounded, like the lavishly entombed pharaohs of ancient Egypt, by several years' of mouth-watering garbage. A vintage 1993 rodent deserved special consideration. I only wish I could have given it. For a number of days, it took the poison I placed in the cupboard under the sink. Then it stopped taking anything. The last I heard of it was a few faint scrabbling noises in the walls of our bedroom one night.

"What's that?" my wife asked anxiously.

"A squirrel hiding peanuts in the eavestrough," I said. It was an honourable lie.

LOVE HURTS

Is there a more reliable sign of spring than the yowls of a pair of cats locked in a primeval Mexican standoff? When it's heard from the shallows of sleep in the middle of the night, the yowling can be mistaken for the cries of an acutely distressed child. It's only after you've fully awakened that you recognize the feline source of this grotesque duet.

When two cats yowl more or less in unison, the effect is not unlike that of the Scottish bagpipe, which seems to make sounds of its own even as it's being played – and often afterward, as the bag slowly empties of air. This is a musical effect that doesn't please all ears equally, and much the same can be said for cat yowling. Animal behaviourists point out that the yowls are not in the least like the tender love songs you often hear in Disney animal movies. In fact, they are part of a highly ritualized territorial battle between two male cats who are vying for the right to mate with a female in heat. If you happen to be awakened by the yowling of only one cat, that's the female in heat summoning all available males to come and fight over her. If you're startled awake by what sounds like a half-dozen or more cats yowling, that's probably the bagpipe your neighbour should know better than to be playing in the middle of the night.

These cat duets are fascinating to listen to, once your ears have become acclimatized to the dissonances. The yowling seems to wax and wane in unison, as though the cats were to some extent performing from a score. The actual sound of an individual yowl is

RAAAAAEEEEEEEEEEEYYYYIIII!!!

Each yowl may undergo numerous modulations of pitch and tone that register even the most subtle changes in a gamut of cat emotions ranging from feverish to frenzied and back again. When the confrontation approaches its climax, the sound of the duet intensifies:

RAAAAAAEEEEEEEEEEEEYAAAIIIIIIIIIIIII!!!!!!

But the above yowl is less common and is usually followed by the sudden flight of one, another or both of the cats.

The bagpipe, by way of contrast, sounds like this:

WEEEEEEEEEEEEEEAAAAAAAAIIIIIIYYYYYYYY!!!

In order to distinguish a bagpipe from a cat yowl, listen carefully for the W sound with which the bagpipe begins.

The most memorable incident of solo female cat yowling I ever heard was from a hotel room in Nice, France, in November of 1980. For several hours, a lone cat in dire romantic straits wailed over and over again. The pathetic sound the cat made that night was:

ELLLP!. . . ELLLLP!. . . ELLLLLP!

One theory advanced by someone in the hotel room in the dead of that sleepless night was that the H sound was absent from the cat's yowl for help because she was a French cat, and therefore not used to pronouncing her H's.

Our own cat was "fixed" at an early age, so she very rarely yowls, except when she's a passenger in an automobile. (I dislike the use of the word "fix" as a euphemism for the de-sexing of animals. The word implies that there was something broken about them that needed repairing, when in fact the problem was that their equipment was in working order.) Instead of yowling at eligible males in springtime, our cat has developed an entirely personal ritual: She maroons herself on our next-door neighbour's roof.

As soon as the last frost has come out of the ground, our cat plots a way to strand herself on the roof and she remains there for hours, meowing pitifully at us to save her. Cats are not very high on my neighbour's list of favourite things, which lends an extra note of urgency to this seasonal psychodrama. The first time our cat wound up on the roof, I discreetly borrowed an extension ladder from another neighbour and tried to rescue her before my next-door neighbour discovered what was going on. Unfortunately, my cat would not co-operate with her rescue. As I teetered on the top rung of the fully extended ladder and called to her, she squirmed delightedly on her back a few tantalizing feet away from me. Apparently she was enjoying my rescue so much that she didn't want it to end. By the time I managed to grab her, a small crowd had formed at the base of the ladder, and the neighbour whose house I had climbed was on her veranda asking, with some justification, what on earth was going on.

The next time our cat marooned herself on our neighbour's roof was the following night, after midnight. The late hour precluded my knocking on the other neighbour's door to borrow his ladder again.

Instead, my wife went out and discreetly tried to reason with the cat, the way a police negotiator might reason with a hostage-taker.

After an epic reasoning session, our cat found her own way down from the roof. We have since concluded that her springtime roof routine is her way of re-enacting the helplessness of kittenhood. It also may be her way of punishing us for "fixing" her and thus robbing her of the chance to yowl in the middle of the night like all the other cats in the neighbourhood.

I wish I had some way of explaining to her that feline sexual relations are overrated. For example, I have no way of pointing out that the reason female cats yowl during the exceedingly brief act of copulation is that the tomcat's sexual organ is equipped with short, sharp spines that point in the opposite direction from which the organ itself points. Getting the action started is not a problem for a pair of cats, but when the tom withdraws from the female, his spines cause the female intense pain.

After I had learned about the peculiar reproductive equipment of toms, our cat's seasonal spell of rooftop isolation took on a new significance. "Fixed" or not, she may simply be waiting for Mr. Spineless to come along.

TEDDY IN THE DEEP FREEZE

I recently underwent an allergy test to determine why I was sneezing thirty and sometimes forty times a day. The test involved having my arm pricked by a multitude of pins containing small quantities of potentially allergenic substances. My only reaction — a mild one, at that — was to dust mites. I asked the doctor where dust mites were usually found, so that I might try to avoid them in the future.

"They're found in dust," she told me.

"That's reasonable," I said, feeling silly for having asked her in the first place.

"They also thrive in carpets, bedsheets and blankets, where they feed on dead human skin cells."

"I see," I said. I hoped that my nodding head and thoughtful expression were camouflaging my shock. Up until that moment, I hadn't realized that my bed was full of dead human skin cells, let alone a multitude of microscopic arthropods who fed on them. (Actually, a travelling vacuum cleaner salesman had tried to clue me into the dead skin cell problem some years ago, but I thought it was just a scare tactic fabricated by the vacuum cleaner company to promote the sale of their product.)

"Most people who have an allergy to dust mites are not allergic to the dust mites per se," the doctor pointed out.

"Thank goodness for that," I said with a nervous chuckle.

"It's when they inhale the fecal matter of dust mites that some people have an allergic reaction," she explained.

"I see," I said, nodding like crazy.

Prior to that day, I had thought of myself as a reasonably tidy and hygiene-conscious individual — not that I had ever been obsessive about cleanliness. But after I had wrapped my mind around the notion that the carpets and beds in my home were crawling with millions of eight-legged, skin-eating creatures who were born, lived, ate, slept and defecated there, and that I regularly inhaled their defecations and sneezed thirty and sometimes forty times a day as a result, it seemed to me that personal hygiene in general had become a moot point.

Since the day of my allergy test, I've tried to keep the subject of dust mites on my mental back burner. Ignorance may not actually be bliss, but sometimes it pays not to know too much about certain things. For instance, I believe it pays not to know that dust mites live in our eyelashes — a tidbit my wife graciously passed along upon my return from the doctor's office. Apparently my wife had known about dust mites and their natural habitat for years, but thought it best that she keep this knowledge to herself.

"My eyelashes?" I said incredulously.

She nodded.

"Right now?"

"As we speak."

"I don't believe you," I said.

"That's just as well. Forget I ever mentioned it."

"That would be easier to do if you hadn't mentioned it."

"You asked," she said.

"So what? I ask all sorts of things."

Ignorance, I have thus proven, is bliss. My wife and I bathe, clean the house and change the bedding on a regular basis. But if I had to get into bed every night with the knowledge that I was joining a legion of parasitic creatures who were dug in for the long haul, there's no way I could sleep as soundly. So I have embraced the Freudian notion of psychological repression on a limited basis and intend, once I have finished writing this gruesome piece, to forget everything I have ever heard about dust mites.

I would advise the same to a group of British pediatricians who suggested that children with asthma or other allergy problems place their teddy bear in the freezer for a few minutes before taking it to bed in order to kill all the dust mites on it. This bizarre strategy may slightly lessen the dust-mite problem for a child — though you can hardly fit the child's entire bed into a freezer, and isn't that where the far greater proportion of the bugs are living? But I have a feeling it's the kind of solution that will only cause more problems.

How, for instance, does a parent go about explaining to a child why Teddy has to be flash-frozen every night before bed? Does the parent dare explain to the child that Teddy is crawling with little eight-legged bugs whose head is attached to their body by a hinge? Does the parent dare tell the child that Teddy is full of these bugs because the child's dead skin cells are all over Teddy? Or does the parent dream up a lame pretext, such as the one that Teddy is in fact a polar bear and therefore enjoys a few minutes on ice before bedtime? Regardless of what explanation is offered, does the parent realistically expect a sensitive child not to bat a mite-infested eyelash at this bizarre antiseptic procedure?

Judging by the degree to which I was attached to my teddy bear when I was young, any attempt by the parent to explain to the child why Teddy must be systematically tortured every evening before bed can only lead to psychological trauma and chronic nightmares. The nightmares will likely revolve around voracious flesh-eating bug-eyed monsters, or the sadistic and unprovoked punishment of teddy bears, or perhaps some horrifying compound of these two themes.

Teddy bears and other stuffed animals are the precious companions who ease a child's nightly descent into the netherworld of darkness, unconsciousness and hallucination. Most grownups aren't overly afraid of going to sleep because they have had time to get used to the idea. Experience has told them that monsters haven't once emerged from any of the closets to cart their sleeping bodies off to a life of terror and servitude in Monsterworld. Grownups know that dreams are the biological equivalent of minor glitches that sometimes show up in a computer's data base if there's a power surge or if the operator of the computer doesn't know what he's doing. A child, on the other hand, hangs on to Teddy for dear life at bedtime because Teddy is the child's only permanent link to the sunny world of wakefulness, and might even be able to ward off the host of night creatures, great and small, who wish to drag the child into an abyss of unspeakable horror.

Surely the prospect of a child retiring for the night in a shaken state, clutching a teddy bear in an advanced stage of rigor mortis, would more than offset any benefit that might result from the freezing of a small percentage of the dust mites that reside on or around the child.

In our effort to purify our children's sleeping environment, let's not throw out the baby with the bathwater and all the ghastly microscopic things floating in it.

PRELUDE TO THE AFTERNOON OF A TADPOLE

The white swan tested the mild breeze with its surprisingly mighty wing span, flapped a number of times to build up some torque, began to sprint on the surface of the water with its spindly legs and eventually lifted off the muddy waters of Cootes Paradise, on the western fringe of Lake Ontario.

The swan didn't attain appreciable altitude. Its two-point landing, about seventy metres east of where it had taken off, was a cartoon-like braking of webbed feet on water. After this brief spurt of activity, the swan settled back into its more familiar pose, afloat on the rippling brown water, its long neck bent in the traditional coat-hanger shape as it drifted serenely beneath the overhanging limbs of a large willow.

I thought to myself: If the white swan realized a popular brand of toilet paper was named after it, and if it were capable of obtaining legal counsel, it would probably sue the toilet paper company for defamation of character.

I immediately wished I hadn't thought that thought. It was inappropriate to the state of the natural world on this balmy spring afternoon, but now I couldn't get it out of my mind. We were watching the swan and the rest of this pastoral tableau from the car, so that Jimmy, our visiting nephew, could listen to his new Ozzy Osbourne tape on the car stereo at the same time. It may have been Mr. Osbourne's music that predisposed me to associate the swan with toilet paper. Heavy metal was not the ideal musical medium with which to savour the languid pleasures of spring. A better choice might have been something by Debussy. But as far as I could tell from his cassette collection, Jimmy wasn't into Debussy.

The swan gazed expectantly at its partner, who hadn't joined it on the short flight and was busy preening itself on the western end of Cootes Paradise. The low-key drama at this point, played out for whoever was inclined to watch, was: Will the one swan fly back to the other, or will the other swan fly back to the one?

Meanwhile, Ozzy Osbourne sang a tune called "Devil's Daughter", in which the object of Mr. Osbourne's affection seemed to be the spawn of Beelzebub or some other vile entity.

"It's kind of dull here," Jimmy said. He was thirteen years old. When I was thirteen years old, I doubt that I would have consented to a modest automobile tour with my aunt and uncle. When I was thirteen, watching a swan float around would have been roughly on a par with watching grass grow, which is exactly what the grass was doing on this fine spring afternoon.

The day before, when the Ozzy Osbourne tape was still safely wrapped in cellophane on a shelf in a downtown record store, we had taken Jimmy up to Crawford Lake to watch sap drip out of maple trees, as though daring him to be bored to death. It was an uncommonly gorgeous Sunday. The watery sap leaking into a shiny metal bucket — plink. . . plink. . . plink. . . — struck me as a miraculous thing. Later, as

Jimmy examined the fossils embedded in just about every rock he happened upon, I watched mesmerized as thousands of tadpoles wriggled in the shallow sunlit water where the ice had begun to retreat. Slowly, inexorably, en masse, the tadpoles were swimming against the mild current toward the mouth of a nearby stream. Many, perhaps most of them, would die in the next few weeks. The tadpoles were untroubled by this fact because they had no inkling of it – or if they did have an inkling, they were plugged so directly into the world that it didn't matter to them.

Jimmy, resplendent in a way in his new Def Leppard T-shirt, two-dollar sunglasses and a Guns 'n' Rose cap, was surprisingly absorbed by his surroundings. If his heavy-metal apparel was meant to make some sort of statement to the world, it wasn't one of which he was conscious as he examined what looked like the tiny spine of some prehistoric organism encrusted in a boulder at the foot of the icebound lake. "Cool," he said, or something to that effect.

Jimmy sang an Ozzy Osbourne song called "Crazy Babies", the subject matter of which I didn't want to know anything about, as we followed a trail gummy with mud and crusted snow into the forest. At one point he stopped singing and pointed to the southwest. The milky imprint of the full moon was faintly visible against the solid blue sky. "It would take only a couple of seconds for a person to die on the moon," Jimmy told us. Then he started singing "Crazy Babies" again and led the way along the trail. We could see he was in a very good mood.

Jimmy chose more sedate attire the following day because he was taking the bus back home that evening. The visit to Cootes Paradise was a last-minute idea, before we drove him to the bus station.

The white swan, after giving up hope of its mate ever joining it, flew back to the centre of the marsh. That's when Jimmy noticed that one of the many Canada geese that were congregating on the grass near the car park was waddling with a pronounced limp as it tried to keep up with its fellow geese. Upon closer inspection, we saw that the goose was missing one of its feet.

My wife felt badly for the goose. She wondered if the rest of the flock shunned it. I said the goose didn't look malnourished, had obviously adjusted to its disability and seemed to be doing fine.

Jimmy, on the other hand, speculated on how the goose had lost its foot. He said some kids he knew were quite capable of taking that goose and cutting off one of its feet without giving the matter a second thought.

I wondered which of our reactions was the most realistic.

Waiting in line to board the bus, Jimmy waved bashfully at us, as though he were already adjusting to the solitude of the journey home. At that moment, for some reason, he reminded me of the tadpoles in the shallows of Crawford Lake.

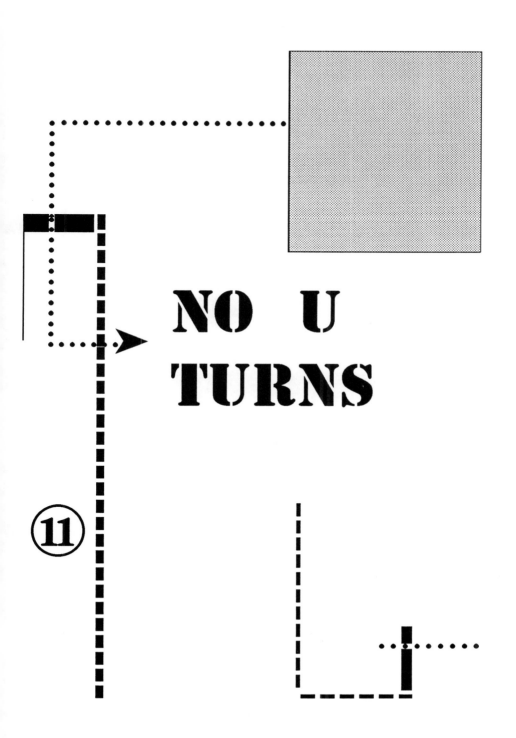

NO U
TURNS

⑪

THE RATTAN CHAIR INCIDENT

Tuesday, 9:07 a.m.: Begin to paint rattan chair. After renovation and painting of room, work on chair seems ideal minor job to use up leftover paint.

10:13 a.m.: Work going more slowly than anticipated. Rattan chair has multitude of nooks and crannies. Also, am applying white paint to previous layer of dark brown paint. Already anticipate need for second coat later on. Drat.

10:52: Ask myself why anyone ever painted rattan chair dark brown in first place. Mood of optimism and good cheer that prevailed at start of job now evaporating.

11:44: Have decided Asian craftspersons who put rattan chair together did so to foil all efforts to paint it. Yet previous coat looks perfect, because was dark. Have formulated general principle of rattan chair painting: Always paint rattan chair darker than existing colour. If existing colour black, leave chair that way or break down into toothpicks or kindling. Never attempt to paint rattan chair white. Unfortunately too late to implement general principle in this case.

12:18 p.m.: Brood about rattan chair while joylessly eating sandwich. Daughter calls. Suggests I use spray paint. Tell her spray paint for sissies. Daughter says spray paint for professionals. Tell her spray paint environmentally unfriendly, plus despise sinister knocking sound when shaking can. Daughter laughs. Doesn't realize situation becoming desperate.

1:31: Have already exceeded by several hours estimated length of job. And have just realized underside of rattan chair will need doing once top side is done. More infernal nooks and crannies. Used to envision hell as place with infinity of empty rooms to be painted. Vision now revised. Hell is place filled with infinite number of dark brown rattan chairs to be painted white, by hand, with a brush, top and bottom.

3:05: Expensive, high-quality paintbrush frayed and bedraggled from endless stabbing at hard-to-get-at places on rattan chair. Notice multitude of white pinpoints on unprotected sections of surrounding carpet from hours of stabbing motion. Make mental note to purchase Varsol and keep wife away from room when she gets home.

4:22: Seventh coffee break of day. Flee upstairs to get away from rattan chair after realization that third coat will be needed. Have not even put first coat on underside of chair. Look up "rattan" in encyclopedia: Climbing palm of tropical Asia, stem noted for extraordinary length, flexible but tough, usually split for weaving baskets. Understand basket-weaving angle perfectly.

5:10: Rattan chair speaks for first time. Says: "You'll never cover me completely." Tell chair: "Oh yeah?" Chair says: "You've left a big gob of dry white paint under my left armrest. You'll have to chip that off with a putty knife, assuming you care at all about your workmanship." Tell chair: "Oh yeah?" Am not surprised rattan chair can speak. Have been expecting it to begin verbally baiting me. Must not rise to bait. Must see task to completion.

5:33: Brief crying jag, interrupted by rattan chair telling me to pull myself together. Wonder if any rattan-painter support groups in Yellow Pages.

5:34: Run to kitchen sink and splash cold water on face. Seem to be losing mind. Must remain focused. Also, must not set paintbrush on counter when splashing cold water on face in future. (Keep wife out of kitchen, too, until Varsol purchased.)

5:36: After doing best to remove paint from kitchen counter, return to find rattan chair has grown. Either that or room has shrunk. Chair says: "I'm feeding on your desperation." Chair is emotional vampire, sapping will to paint. Am woozy. Need more coffee.

5:39: Can hear rattan chair's derisive voice from kitchen. Try not to listen as coffee brews. Wonder if can reach hardware store before closing time, buy case of spray paint, spray living daylights out of rattan chair. Chair now making sounds like little girl in movie, *Exorcist*.

5:59: Wife not home for while yet. Could reduce rattan chair to fine pulp with small industrial grinder, tell wife donated chair to Salvation Army. Or could weave chair into nice basket. Wife likes baskets.

8:30: Delirious but still painting. Chair has quieted down. Am gaining ground on it. Say to chair: "I'm feeding on your desperation now." Chair replies: "On the contrary. I kind of like this new colour."

8:37: Pry open old can of dayglo orange paint found in basement. My mission clear now.

EDUCATING JOHNNIE

Every September, when the shadows lengthen, the temperatures dip and the leaves begin to turn, my heart goes out to the students of the world. I know that some students — especially the older ones, who have some say in the course of their affairs — probably relish the prospect of returning to their studies. I'm not concerned about them. My compassion is reserved for those students who dread the onset of September as deeply as I did when I was their age. I watch these students trudge off to school and I can tell from their body language that all the crisp scribblers, sharp pencils, fancy duo-tangs and packets of reinforcements in the world can't possibly compensate for the sweet freedom of which they have been arbitrarily robbed. As I watch these students, I say to myself: "There, but for the grace of the fact that I have already gone, go I."

My early education was punctuated by the annual autumnal tragedy of losing my geometry set, which I had purchased scant days before from the office supply store. Once I lost track of my compass, protractor, ruler and other tools of the geometric trade, I knew that the school year had begun its seemingly inevitable decline to half-finished homework assignments and involuntary naps in math class. The geometry set, my virgin eraser, my gleaming package of Laurentian colouring pencils, my stiff new schoolbag redolent of animal hide — all were symbols of the best intentions with which I began every school year. The road to St. Mary's School was paved with them.

In my elementary school days I was unable to articulate fully my dislike of organized education, so I just stayed in bed as long as I could on those shockingly dark September mornings. By the time I reached high school I was somewhat more articulate, so I would stay in bed as long as I could, then I would subject whoever was within earshot to a tirade on the evils of a standardized curriculum. The net effect was of course the same: I wound up slumped over my standardized desk in a blindingly fluorescent classroom with the webbed skin between my thumb and index finger caught in the jaws of my stiff new ring binder. I learned a valuable lesson in the process, but I can't for the life of me recall what it was.

Of all the courses of instruction I was subjected to in high school, the one I dreaded the most was physical education. This was not because I was innately afraid of being physically educated so much as the fact that we were made to perform cruel and unusual activities in that course in those days. One such activity was crab soccer, which consisted of scuttling crab-like on one's hands and feet along the gymnasium floor while purporting to chase a soccer ball. I didn't understand why I had to play crab soccer whereas the girls got to fox-trot with one another in their physical education class. It seemed to me that doing the fox trot with a girl in bloomers would have been far more physically educational for boys than pretending they were crustaceans. I couldn't see how pretending I was a crustacean prepared me in any way for adult life — unless I were contemplating a career in politics, which I wasn't.

Once we had exhausted the educational ramifications of crab soccer to the phys ed teacher's satisfaction, we moved on to the most appalling program of all: gymnastics. This part of the curriculum was based on the entirely erroneous proposition that all young people should be willing and able to vault over pommel horses, suspend themselves inside and above parallel bars, and generally defy the laws of thermodynamics. In my case, the gymnastics program was mainly an opportunity to humiliate myself in front of my peers. Thank goodness the girls were too busy fox-trotting with one another to watch me fling my less than nimble self over wooden horses and grimly apply tons of talcum powder to my armpits in anticipation of my inevitable premature "dismount" from the parallel bars.

One year, I managed to be excused from gymnastics after I sprained my wrist while performing a pommel vault. (Actually, it was a wrench more than a sprain. (Actually, it was a twist more than a wrench. (Actually, it was hardly anything at all, but I nevertheless bound my wrist in an elastic bandage and received a *to whom it may concern* note from my family doctor suggesting that the wrist would need at least four weeks to heal completely. (My doctor was a compassionate man.))))

Prior to the incident on the pommel horse, I had privately explored ways in which I could be excused from phys ed by a doctor's note without having any of my extra-curricular activities curtailed. At one point, I considered telling my doctor I had a pathological fear of taking a shower in a group setting, in the hope that he would draft a note along these lines to the phys ed teacher. I abandoned the plan at the last minute, after I envisioned my classmates speculating at length and aloud on the reason for my fear of taking a shower in a group setting.

The greatest medical note ever proffered on my behalf was written by an officious school nurse at St. Mary's when I was in grade four. The nurse's note said, more or less: "This student cannot attend class for an indefinite period on account of he has a pimple on his forehead." I had no idea why a pimple on my forehead was grounds for a prolonged holiday, and I certainly wasn't about to ask. Oddly enough, neither did the authorities at St. Mary's.

I vividly recall the elation with which I trotted off to a park with my football on the afternoon of my release from school. I pictured my classmates toiling away at long division as I kicked the football in the full flush of health in the middle of the week. I wasn't in the least bit upset about the pimple on my forehead. I was ten years old, so acne didn't yet have the power to horrify.

A policeman on a foot beat happened to observe me frolicking alone with my football. (This was back in the days when patrolling the streets in search of truant schoolchildren was a key component of community police work.) The policeman sauntered over to me, his impressive holster level with my eyes, and asked me what I was doing out of school.

"I can't be in school on account of I have a pimple on my forehead," I said, pointing to the blemish.

"Really?" said the policeman.

"I have a note from the nurse," I told him. "She said I can't go back to school until the pimple goes away. Can I see your gun?"

"Are you telling the truth?" the policeman asked.

"I am! The nurse told the school they would either have to send everybody home except me, or they would have to send me home until the pimple went away. So that's what they did. Can I see your gun?"

"Then why aren't you at home?" the policeman said.

"The fresh air is good for the pimple," I told him, rising giddily to the occasion. "The nurse said it will heal more quickly if I'm outside. Can I see your gun?"

"I'm busy," the policeman said, moving away.

This was my ultimate triumph. Not only had a single pimple sprung me from school, it had also stymied the forces of law and order. "Bring on the pimples," I said to the sky. And they came. But apparently the pimples I got in high school were not the contagious kind, which partly explains why I wound up having to take so many showers in a group setting.

By the time I reached university, I found it very difficult to focus on strictly academic pursuits. As a student in the fine arts faculty of a major Ontario university in the early 1970s, when education had a rather elastic quality and the minds of many people were similarly stretched for one reason or another, I discovered that the subject matter of some of my courses overlapped. Pressed for time on one occasion, I took the risk of submitting the same paper to two different professors. One of the professors taught an introductory first-year course, the other a second-year course. The professor of the introductory course gave me a B for the paper. The professor of the second-year course gave me an A. This in itself was educational.

One of the courses I was obliged to take in my first year was a Humanities course entitled "Problems in Contemporary Culture." This course was taught by a youngish woman who lectured in a floor-length raccoon coat. One day, the woman gave us a slide show and asked us to comment on the photographs. She was especially interested in our observations on the photographer's "decapitation obsession", since many of the slides omitted the tops of people's heads. (I thought they were just inept photographs. I had so much to learn in those days.)

The woman in the raccoon coat lingered an especially long time over a slide depicting a man harpooning a fish from the side of a boat. She asked the class: "Which would you rather be: the fish or the man?"

"The man?" one student answered uncertainly and the slide show continued.

Looking back on that quintessential moment of my formal education, and the panoply of pedagogues who preceded the woman in the raccoon coat, I realize now that they and I were Problems in Contemporary Culture.

LET GO

One of the few positive consequences of the two recessions of recent years is the wealth of new workplace euphemisms for losing one's job. Just as the Inuit are said to have a multitude of words to describe the various kinds of snow they must put up with on a virtually year-round basis in the Arctic, we now have a rich pool of words and terms to draw from in describing the various ingenious ways in which persons can be separated from their livelihood.

Although it's somewhat hard to believe, previous generations had only one or two terms to denote the sudden and usually unpleasant experience of losing one's job. The most common word was the verb "fire". If you were the person losing your job, you were "fired" from it, as in: "Honey, I've been fired." If you were the management official making the decision, you "fired" someone, as in: "Honey, you're fired."

At some point during the recession of the early 1980s, there was a general agreement that the verb "fire" implied too much violence and ruthlessness on the part of the people doing the firing. Although the exact roots of this usage are uncertain, it's believed the term arose either from the medical practice of cauterizing, which is the burning away of tissue to prevent bleeding ("I see no Harm in Firing or Cauterizing Young Colts." – Bracken, 1750), or from the practice of driving animals from a place by setting the place on fire ("He shall bring a brand from heaven and fire us hence, like horses." – Shake-speare, 1605).

The fact that these uses of the verb "fire" seemed to apply mainly to barnyard animals may also have influenced the decision in many management circles in the early 80s to replace it with the more humane and efficient-sounding verb, "terminate". This was a fine choice at first glance, since it clearly evoked the unequivocal nature of losing one's job. (The Oxford English Dictionary definition of "terminate" leaves little doubt as to its meaning: "To bring to an end, put an end to, to cause to cease, to end.") It might have remained the most popular word to describe the sudden onset of unemployment had it not been for the discovery that intelligence organizations such as the CIA had for years been using this verb as a euphemism for assassination. Soon the search was on for a kinder, gentler euphemism.

By the time the second recession struck in the early 1990s, corporations were armed with a host of terms to help cushion the blow of virtually all forms of job loss. Companies "downsized" (got rid of great numbers of employees) in response to tough economic conditions. If they didn't downsize, they "reorganized" (got rid of great numbers of employees), "streamlined" (got rid of great numbers of employees), "rationalized" (got rid of great numbers of employees) or underwent a period of "negative growth" (got rid of great numbers of employees).

The large-scale bloodletting of the second recession unfolded in an elegant language that seemed to imply astute captaincy rather than the willy-nilly deployment of lifeboats. A kind of human salvage industry known as "outplacement" grew and prospered as the numbers of men and women abandoned at sea continued to rise and as companies looked for more painless ways to jettison them. Highly paid outplacement consultants came into the workplace and advised companies on how many people to get rid of, and which euphemisms to use when they did so. Then these same consultants advised outplaced employees on the best ways to find work with companies the consultants had not yet done any consulting for.

But as the economy slowly began to climb out of the recession, the outplacement industry found that it, too, was being outplaced. Many of these companies were forced to downsize to reflect the lower incidence of downsizing in the workplace as a whole. Like Count Dracula, who must retreat to his coffin when the sun comes up, the outplacement industry instinctively recoils from brightening prospects.

All in all, the simple terminology of yesteryear is no longer adequate to describe the intricate operations of today's economy. And since it's generally conceded that employment levels may never return to what they were before the ravages of the past fifteen years regardless of how the economy fares, the future of euphemisms looks extremely promising.

THE MAN WHO SHOPPED FOR SOFTWARE

A friend of his, who knew more about these things than he did, told him the information highway was not a highway in the sense that an actual highway was a highway, but it was nevertheless a good idea to be aware of road conditions before setting out on it. "If you can't speak the language of the people who sell the computers," his friend said, "how can you possibly get what you're looking for?"

"All I want is some word-processing software," he scoffed. "It's not like I'm shopping for a whole computer or anything."

"Your system is years out of date," his friend told him. "You won't understand what they're talking about unless you bone up a little."

"Nonsense," he said. "I'm reasonably intelligent, and the people in the store are paid to instruct and inform me."

"Don't be a fool," his friend warned him.

Perhaps if he had known exactly how outdated his present home computer system was, he wouldn't have ignored his friend's advice. The reason he was shopping for new software was that his present software had for some reason become incompatible with seemingly every other computer system on the information highway. This alone should have convinced him that a lot of traffic had overtaken him in recent years. Instead, he marched blithely into a computer store, expecting to be tolerated by the superior beings who worked there.

"I would like a new software package for my PC, preferably Word Perfect 6.1," he said to the young clerk behind the counter. He had rehearsed this opening line several times in front of a full-length mirror at home before trying it out in public. It sounded very convincing.

"Do you have Windows?" the clerk asked him.

"Why?" he said. "Can't I bring the software home through the front door?"

The clerk didn't laugh at this. Laughter, however derisive, would have been preferable to a blank stare, which was the clerk's only reaction.

"I don't have Windows," he finally confessed to the clerk.

"Okay," the clerk said. "That complicates it a bit."

"I do have DOS," he told the clerk, making a wild guess that Windows and DOS were somehow variations on the same thing, though he hadn't the slightest notion what that thing might be.

"What kind of drive do you have?" the clerk wanted to know.

He tried not to blink. "I, uh. . ."

The clerk stared remorselessly at him.

"Tell me," he said to the clerk, "what exactly do you mean by drive?"

He was now officially stranded on the information highway, marooned on the shoulder of the cyberspace road with an empty gas tank. His friend had been right after all. His heart sunk even more when he realized that he knew as little about the vehicles with which he travelled on actual highways as he did about the metaphorical ones with which he lurched through the electronic ether of the information highway. He was a hazard to all other motorists. He should have been pulled over long ago.

Just then, from the jaws of humilation, he snatched a desperate idea: Perhaps information of any kind could serve as fuel on the information highway. Perhaps even malarkey, a lesser-known information byproduct, would work. If he was out of gas, why couldn't he simply manufacture some of his own? He decided to put this theory to the test at once.

"My computer uses the larger discs," he said to the clerk. "The ones that have a hole in the centre, like a square forty-five record."

"Forty-five?" said the clerk.

"You know: The little discs you can stack on your portable output system. They replaced seventy-eights."

The clerk had a perplexed look on his face for the first time that afternoon — perhaps for the first time in his life. "You mean CD-ROM?"

"Heavens, no," he said with a chuckle. "I'm talking about analog discs, made of black vinyl. The information is stored on a spiral groove etched directly onto the vinyl. You access the data by using a small diamond stylus — or a roofing nail, if your stylus is worn out — to convert the data into electrical impulses and feed it through a transducer into the output console."

A relieved smile appeared on the clerk's face. "Now I know what you're talking about. You mean the new generation of CD-sized laser video discs that are just coming on the market."

"Please!" he said in an offended tone of voice. A number of other customers in the store looked over to see what was going on. "The system I'm talking about doesn't stoop to simplistic digital solutions. Some of it isn't even electrical. I'm talking about the cutting edge, boy. I have a Victrola unit at home that's manually powered. It works like a charm, and it isn't affected by variations in power allotment from the various utilities. Have you not heard of any of this?"

The clerk looked at him, then at the slowly gathering audience, and whispered: "How many megabytes per second?"

"You poor, misinformed fellow," he sighed. "I'm not talking about megabytes per second. I'm talking about revolutions per minute! RPM. It's going to transform the way we do things."

"I'll have to ask the manager about it when he gets back from lunch," the clerk said hesitantly.

"Do that. And while you're at it, ask him if he knows anything about direct hard-copy graphite rod word-processing systems."

"What?" said the clerk.

"You haven't heard about that?"

The clerk shook his head.

He took a deep, patient breath. "Instead of a cursor or mouse, you use a small pointed rod of graphite encased in wood to store information of all kinds directly onto any solid data base. You can buy a graphite rod for mere pennies, and you just throw it away when it's done. The graphite rod is so simple that even the youngest child can use it. And for slightly more than the cost of a graphite rod you can get a paper notebook with tremendous memory capacity. The whole system is completely portable. You don't even need a power supply."

"Amazing," the clerk said. Several of the store's customers, who had gathered near the counter by now, shook their head in agreement.

"And that's not all," he said. "I've heard about some recent experiments with an ink-based data delivery system that would last much longer than the average graphite rod, and ring binders that could store twenty times as much memory as a standard notebook. And you dare to waste my time with talk of Windows and CD-ROM."

"I'm so sorry," the clerk said. "I didn't know about all these advances."

"You've got to make it your business to know, son. Why don't I drop by in a few days and show you and your manager what a graphite rod data system can do for a fraction of the cost of any of the things in here?"

"Would you do that?" the clerk said.

"Absolutely," he said. "All scientific breakthroughs belong to the whole world. Only with the free and unfettered exchange of information can the new electronic world order come into being."

Just then, a young boy who had been scanning the video-game rack stepped up to him, tugged on his sleeve and said, "Hey Mister, are you from the twenty-first century or something?"

"I've got to go now," he said to the awestruck boy, the clerk and everyone else in the computer store that afternoon on the information highway. "Keep up the good work here." Then he swept out of the store.

He had proven his friend wrong. He didn't have any new software to show for his efforts, but he was nevertheless in the fast lane again, running on empty with the cybernetic wind blowing through his virtual hair.

ONE HUNDRED YEARS OF CRACKER JACKS

In June of 1993, without any of the pomp and circumstance that usually mark major cultural milestones, Cracker Jacks turned one hundred years old. The fact that no one bothered to make much of this centennial shows the extent to which Cracker Jacks have become woven into the fabric of our lives. More than a century after its invention, we take this fabled food product for granted.

From a nutritionally correct perspective, popcorn encased in a shellac of sugar and corn syrup may seem an insubstantial or even unsalutary snack. But who among us can't recall the specific texture and flavour of a mouthful of them? I haven't tasted Cracker Jacks in at least two decades, yet I believe I can recreate the sensation in precise detail: Extract all the water from a vat of industrial-strength cola, pour popcorn into the remaining treacle, stir the mixture, let it harden, carefully remove it from the vat and eat it. It's a sticky, poppy, taffy, corny, treacly taste sensation.

In these health-conscious times, there's a tendency to underestimate F.W. Rueckheim's achievement when he introduced Cracker Jacks at the 1893 World Exposition in Chicago. His product was an instant hit, even though Rueckheim didn't yet have a name for it. Several years later, according to legend, a travelling salesman tasted Rueckheim's famous collation and exclaimed: "That's a cracker jack!" The salesman's exclamation, in the quaint colloquial idiom of the period, meant that he thought popcorn coated with a shellac of sugar and corn syrup was groovy.

As of 1908, when Albert Von Tilzer composed "Take Me Out to the Ball Game" with its famous line about buying "some peanuts and Cracker Jack", Rueckheim's product became inextricably linked with baseball. In 1912, Rueckheim further sealed Cracker Jacks' place in history by offering a little prize in each package of the product. The prizes reflected the changes in popular culture over the years: There were war-related prizes in the 1940s, cowboy-related prizes in the '50s and flower child-related prizes in the '60s. Not having purchased Cracker Jacks in the ensuing decades, I can only surmise that scale-model ugly clothing prizes were offered in the '70s, and toy BMWs in the '80s.

In the interest of impartial journalism, I went out the other night and bought a box of Cracker Jacks. I was immediately struck by a number of things:

1. The product is called Cracker Jack, not Cracker Jacks, as most of us seem to think.

2. I wasn't surprised that the price of the product had grown, but the box containing the Cracker Jack seems to have shrunk.

3. Below the Cracker Jack logo is a subtitle that states, "Caramel-coated popcorn and peanuts." Prior to reading that subtitle, I hadn't realized that there were peanuts in a box of Cracker Jack. Although the number of peanuts is not what you would call appreciable, Albert von Tilzer nevertheless should have amended the lyrics to his famous song to reflect this fact. The redundant phrase, "Buy me some peanuts and Cracker Jack" easily could have been changed to, "Buy me a box of that Cracker Jack." Then again, perhaps by separating the peanuts from the Cracker Jack in his song, von Tilzer was making a sly comment on the relative dearth of peanuts in Cracker Jack. Since von Tilzer is no longer with us, we will never know for sure.

4. The "surprise" inside the box of Cracker Jack I purchased was a small rainbow sticker which I was encouraged to apply to my skin or clothes. I have no idea in what way a rainbow reflects popular culture in the 1990s.

5. A notice on the side of the box informs me that for $5.95 plus applicable sales tax, I can send away for a Cracker Jack wristwatch.

6. The two principal ingredients of Cracker Jack are sugar and corn syrup, not popcorn and peanuts.

7. Sugar and corn syrup are not bad at all on popcorn.

8. When you've finished eating your Cracker Jack, you can poke your nose into the empty box and smell the remains of your childhood.

PROCEED WITH CAUTION

⑫

THE BEGINNING OF THE YEAR

Prior to the middle of the eighteenth century, the English-speaking world celebrated New Year's Day on March 25. This may explain why so many of us wake up on the morning of January 1 with a general feeling of disorientation, a splitting headache, loose bowels, short-term amnesia, a heightened sensitivity to light, and the telephone number of a person named Candy on a matchbook in the pocket of our coat, which we for some reason wore to bed.

The simple explanation for this confused state is that we still haven't entirely adjusted to the transfer of New Year's Day from March to January. Some bewilderment is bound to persist, just as our biological clocks have trouble shifting from standard time to daylight-saving time and back again in the spring and fall. Further complicating our ability to grasp when New Year's Day occurs is the fact that the Jewish new year begins in early autumn, the Chinese new year begins anytime from January 10 to February 19, and the new fiscal year, with which accountants solemnly mark the progress of our indebtedness, begins in spring.

Under the primitive Roman calendar, the New Year began on March 25, at more or less the time of the first full moon after the spring equinox. Ancient Romans might nevertheless have thrown a party on the evening of December 31, since they fervently believed in the principle of having a good time. The only problem was that there was no such date on their calendar. December had only twenty-nine days at the time, and it was followed immediately by the month of March.

In the seventh century BC, the Etruscan king Numa Pompilius added the months of January and February to the calendar to help it conform to the cycle of the seasons. But the Romans disliked this innovation and threw January and February out of their calendar in 510 BC. Three hundred and fifty years later, the two months were put back in again, by which time the people of Rome were understandably unsure of what date it was. Then, on the advice of an astronomer, Julius Caesar further confused matters by adding ninety days to the year 46 BC and changing the length of most of the months. The year 46 BC, which wound up being four hundred and forty-five days long, was referred to by the Romans as *ultimus annus confusionus,* which translates roughly as "major disturbance of the rectum".

It wasn't until the adoption of the Gregorian calendar that New Year's Day was moved from March 25 to January 1. This change occurred in 1582 in most of continental Europe, but England and its colonies held out until 1752, Russia and Finland until 1918, Greece until 1923, and the province of Newfoundland remains a half-hour out of step.

Although the tradition of celebrating the New Year on January 1 is a relatively recent one, the custom of making personal resolutions at the start of the year is as old as the hills. It probably stretches as far back as the first self-improvement instincts of our ape-like ancestors, who had ample potential for improvement. For all we know, the decision of one such ape-like individual to stop walking around on all fours was a New Year's resolution.

Of all the milestones with which we mark the passage of time, New Year's Day is the most laden with notions of personal betterment. What's touching about New Year's resolutions is that they're generally rooted in kindness and humility. You rarely hear of anyone resolving to become a more rapacious slumlord in the new year, or to find more effective ways of alienating the rest of humanity. By and large, people want to make their presence on earth more positive and life-enhancing. For this reason, they should be given every opportunity to grow into the role of a better person, rather than be expected to change substantially at the stroke of midnight on New Year's Eve. Rome wasn't renovated in a day.

On the first of January, the world's odometer clicks ahead one digit, thereby reducing the resale value of us all. As with people who sell previously-owned cars for a living, our first inclination may be to look for quick ways to repair rust, metal fatigue and a gear box that doesn't always rise to the occasion. One stratagem, which is illegal in the automotive trade, is to rewind the odometer to a more flattering mileage count. But this ruse has no practical application to the passage of time. At the current stage of our technological development, we simply don't have the tools to make time go backward. It moves inexorably, remorselessly forward, like a lineup at Canada Customs.

The trick to starting the new year on the right foot is to make a clean break from the personal impediments of the past. The trick to making a clean break from the personal impediments of the past is to give oneself the necessary time to work up that steam to do so. Think of a year of life in terms of the movement of a pendulum. Think of the first few days of January as that brief period of apparent immobility when the pendulum has reached its furthest point from the centre of its arc. This apparent immobility is in fact an intrinsic part of the pendulum's overall motion. Dangle a necklace or other chain in front of your eyes and swing it back and forth. If you still don't grasp my pendulum illustration, you might at the very least put yourself into a pleasant hypnotic trance. I'm not suggesting a pleasant hypnotic trance is the ideal way to pass the first few days of a new year, but I'm not *not* suggesting it, either.

We can all draw inspiration from our ape-like ancestors. Despite their hopelessly primitive circumstances, they believed the future was worth investing in. So they started chipping stones and bones with which to assail the members of rival groups and other animals. They discovered fire and the wheel and they moved from the treetops to the cave. On the walls of the cave they painted artful depictions of the humans and animals they hoped to assail in the coming days and weeks. They watched the sun and moon and stars and were filled with perplexing questions, such as why they went blind after watching the sun for too long, whereas watching the stars for long periods was perfectly okay. They noticed the passage of the seasons and thought that it seemed like only yesterday they were wrapping themselves in the hide of the woolly mammoth to keep warm. Could it already be that time of year again?

Inspired to act by something intangibly human on a long-ago New Year's Day, one of our forward-looking ancestors finally stopped walking around on all fours, stood up tall and said aloud, albeit in a series of grunts: "I can see all the way to Zorg's place from up here."

REVERSAL OF FORTUNE

This is an open letter to the person whose claim to an eighteen million-dollar Michigan state lottery jackpot recently elapsed:

Dear sir or madam,

Congratulations. You are a living worst-case scenario. By purchasing a jackpot-winning lottery ticket and either misplacing it or forgetting about it, you have transcended mere bad luck and ventured into previously uncharted realms of misfortune. Your achievement is awe-inspiring.

Since the chances of winning a lottery are frequently compared to those of being struck by lightning, let's pursue the metaphor: Let's picture you as a person who was struck by lightning but was unaffected by the experience and — here's where your accomplishment truly staggers the mind — *you never even noticed.*

Although you're a living worst-case scenario, you remain unaware of this fact. Perhaps you read the article in the Detroit Free Press about the deadline having passed for collecting the eighteen million-dollar jackpot and you said to yourself, "What a miserable schmuck that person must be. Thank God I always keep track of the lottery tickets I buy."

Buy you didn't keep track of all the lottery tickets you bought, and in so doing you have taught us all a very important lesson by showing the true odds against winning a lottery jackpot. For years, the slogan of one of the seemingly infinite number of lotteries operating up here in Canada was that you couldn't win if you didn't buy a ticket. This slogan was designed to compel the public to conclude by deductive reasoning that

(a) they could win if they did buy a ticket, therefore

(b) they better as hell buy a ticket.

You, sir or madam, have exposed the faulty logic of that slogan by demonstrating that one can actually buy the winning ticket in an eighteen million-dollar state lottery and still not win the lottery.

In the early days of publicly administered lotteries (it used to be called the numbers racket before governments muscled the Mob out of the action), I remember worrying more than once about losing or accidentally destroying my lottery ticket, since it was potentially the most valuable of all my personal effects. It occurred to me back then that the only safe place for a lottery ticket until the day of the draw was in a bank safety deposit box. Even that strategy wasn't entirely fool-proof, since banks and trust companies sometimes went under, taking their depositors with them. But to carry a live lottery ticket in one's wallet, or to stick it on the refrigerator with a magnet in the shape of Tweetie Pie, was potentially as great a folly as carrying several million dollars in cash in your wallet, or scotch-taping the money to your fridge and other appliances for safekeeping.

Over the years, what with the high proportion of losing tickets to winning tickets and the preponderance of winning tickets whose prize consisted of the privilege of acquiring another losing ticket free of charge, we've all become more laissez-faire about the lottery tickets we buy. We're still interested in holding onto our tickets until the day of the draw, but they don't have quite the magic of those early tickets, so we sometimes lose track of them. Owning a losing lottery ticket is a minor form of bad luck. Losing track of such a ticket is marginally less lucky. But losing track of an eighteen million-dollar ticket, as you did, is the mark of a quantum loser who has taken the dumb luck of the world on his shoulders in a messianic effort to cleanse us all. You deserve our reverence as much as our sympathy.

It's impossible to explain why certain random things happen to certain individuals. For example, in the autumn of 1994 a chunk of frozen urine crashed through the roof of a Thornhill, Ontario couple's home. Authorities were able to trace the urine to a Korean Air jetliner which passed directly over Thornhill on the day in question. Airlines are customarily prohibited from "releasing" any materials from their aircraft in the air. But a seal in the Korean aircraft's toilet apparently failed, causing the urine to leak out. The urine froze into a large chunk when it came into contact with the cold air, and the chunk crashed through the roof of the Thornhill couple's house.

When I heard about the incident, I asked myself: Why their roof? Why not mine? Why is life, for want of a more sensitive word under the circumstances, a crapshoot?

Over the years, mathematicians have attempted to refine notions of chance and luck into the more empirical concept of probability.

Their efforts have yielded interesting equations such as this one, which I would explain to you if I knew the first thing about it.

$$P(n,r)= \frac{n!}{(n-r)!}$$

The science of probability builds statistical forms out of data derived from samples. For example, by determining the number of persons who bought a Michigan lottery ticket, and collating that figure with the number of persons who won the eighteen million-dollar jackpot and the number of persons who neglected to claim the jackpot, mathematicians are able to conclude with reasonable certainty that you, sir or madam, are an exceptionally unlucky individual.

May I offer a few practical suggestions?

If you should wake up in the middle of the night and suddenly recall having purchased a ticket for the Michigan state lottery draw whose jackpot eligibility recently elapsed, heat a cup of milk, take whatever strong medication is at hand and for heaven's sake go back to sleep.

If you're foolish enough to check the winning numbers in the aforementioned lottery, and you happen to notice that the winning numbers correspond to the birth dates of you, your spouse and your two children, and that you've faithfully played these numbers whenever you've bought a lottery ticket over the past twelve years, ask your doctor for a referral to a qualified hypnotherapist in order to have this memory wiped from your brain.

Whatever you do, don't go rooting through the pockets of any shirts, jackets and trousers you haven't worn in a while. Any discovery you might make would be counter-productive at this stage.

And finally, please bear this in mind: Those who cannot remember the old saying that "those who cannot remember the past are doomed to repeat it" are doomed to have the old saying repeated to them.

THREE HORSEMEN OF THE APOCALYPSE

Scientific breakthroughs occur with such frequency on the information highway that some of them don't receive the attention they deserve. A case in point is a ground-breaking 1992 study by Jonathan Shedler, professor of clinical psychology at the Institute of Advanced Psychological Studies in Garden City, New Jersey. Dr. Shedler's study concluded that even if people believe they're happy, they may in fact be concealing distress that will one day result in a heart attack.

In the course of his research, Dr. Shedler discovered that people who were hiding psychological distress from themselves displayed an unusual jump in heartbeat and blood pressure whenever they performed stressful tasks. This jump in heartbeat placed an undue strain on the cardiovascular system that would have been immediately noticeable to miserable people, since they are always on the lookout for ways to validate their distress. But it would have gone unnoticed and untreated by people who mistakenly think they're happy, thus further jeopardizing their health.

What troubled me most about Dr. Shedler's findings were not their physiological implications, but rather the notion that we can dupe ourselves into believing we're happy-go-lucky individuals, when in fact we're in a state of distress that will become a major factor in the heart disease that ultimately kills us.

The notion of hidden distress points to one of the most potentially distressing question of our time: How can we tell the difference between true happiness and elaborately camouflaged dejection? On our wedding day, even though my wife and I seemed from the video and photographic evidence to be fluorescent with joy, had the seeds of despondency already been planted? If we were to become filthy-rich, would the unconscious awareness that we couldn't possibly live long enough to spend all the money begin to accumulate like cholesterol in the narrowest stretches of our psychological arteries?

The mere asking of questions such as these lends them a legitimacy they would not otherwise have. This is why Dr. Shedler's 1992 study, which was carried in brief by a number of news organizations and then ignored, should have been refuted then and there. Not having been refuted, the study has undoubtedly taken up residence in that part of our collective psyche where similarly distressing fragments of information hide until they can coalesce into globules of raw malaise.

And so to refute: Either a person is happy or a person is not. This isn't something over which we should be splitting hairs. Questioning the authenticity of one's happiness has essentially the same psychological effect as watching someone sneeze into a salad bar: It makes one wary and mistrustful. Among other things, it makes one wonder why Dr. Shedler chose this area of psychological research in the first place. Could it be that Dr. Shedler had developed misgivings about the legitimacy of his own happiness, so he worked out a scientific system by which he could drag the rest of us down into his personal sinkhole of self-doubt? Or is my suspicion about Dr. Shedler's motives merely another consequence of the hidden distress that has secretly choreographed my every move since birth?

George Bernard Shaw once said, "We have no more right to consume happiness without producing it than to consume wealth without producing it." I wish Dr. Shedler had pinned a copy of Shaw's injunction on his office wall before undertaking his research. The same goes for a cardiologist by the name of Alan Wilson. He's the author of a 1993 study which concluded that men are twenty percent more likely to have a heart attack on their birthday than on any other day of the year.

Even if this statistic were true – which it probably is on some level or other – it ill-behooved Dr. Wilson to share the information with the rest of the world. Speaking for myself as a man, I don't want to know what my chances are of having a heart attack on my birthday compared to the rest of the year. Even if my chances are one hundred percent better, it's not as though I can avoid the day. So why ruin my enjoyment of the double-fudge brownie cake my daughter customarily bakes me, even if the more prudent course of action would be to hammer a couple of candles into a Melba toast?

Dr. Wilson arrived at his findings after studying the records of more than one hundred thousand heart attacks treated at ninety New Jersey hospitals over a five-year period. He attributed the higher incidence of heart attacks on birthdays – twenty-one percent for men, nine percent for women –to the emotional stress and physical overindulgence that often accompany their celebration. Implicit in his conclusion was the fact that the emotional stress of a birthday naturally increases as one progresses through life, since few of us are ever delighted about the fact that we're another year older. Many people attempt to treat this stress by overindulging in food and drink, thereby increasing their chances of being not only a year older, but mortally ill.

The only positive outcome of Dr. Wilson's study is that it might encourage people who are celebrating their birthday to try to avoid becoming unduly stressed or indulged on that day. But this potential benefit is far outweighed by the fact that the mere publication of Dr. Wilson's findings has made birthdays far more stressful than they were before he poked his nose into the subject.

Rounding out our survey of depressing medical breakthroughs is the work of Howard Friedman. He's the psychologist who oversaw a recent long-term study of human longevity which concluded that cheerfulness in childhood contributes to a shorter life span.

Dr. Friedman reported to the American Psychological Association that of all the personality traits of childhood, only cheerfulness and low conscientiousness seemed to have a measurable effect on the length of a person's life — and neither of the effects was positive. Thanks to Dr. Friedman's study, we are now able to add cheerfulness to the growing list of genetic and behavioural markers with which to gauge exactly how nasty, brutish and short we can expect our life to be.

Dr. Friedman has torn the lid off childhood cheerfulness and exposed it for what it is: a futile attempt to hide the lethal distress which Dr. Shedler says is lurking behind many happy faces — especially during their birthday celebration, which Dr. Wilson believes to be less than a complete party without someone from the coroner's office standing by.

For this, doctors, thanks a heap.

A NOEL STORY

It was the night before Christmas and everything was so perfect at Noel's house that Noel was beginning to have grave doubts about it.

His son, Emmanuel, had gone up to bed at eight-thirty without even a token protest. Normally there was no way of subduing the boy until ten at the earliest on Christmas Eve. Noel's wife, Beth, was in the kitchen whipping up a couple of hot toddies. Beth had never made hot toddies before on Christmas Eve. In past years, she and Noel heated some store-bought egg nog in the microwave oven, spread Emmanuel's presents under the tree, commented on the store-bought egg nog's eerie resemblance to Milk of Magnesia, then called it a night. This year, for some reason, everything was different.

While Beth puttered in the kitchen, Noel went to the living room window and watched unusually large flakes of snow fall lazily to earth. The night was otherwise still. The fresh snow already blanketing the rooftops, tree limbs and shrubs of his neighbourhood looked pristine as cotton batten. Turning away from the window, Noel noticed for the first time that instead of the tangled mess of mostly burnt-out lights that customarily adorned the family Christmas tree, actual candles were casting a lovely, warm glow throughout the room. The jarring sight of the candles on the tree led to a more alarming realization: There were no presents under the tree, no presents hidden in any of the closets, no presents anywhere in the house. Apparently he and Beth had completely forgotten to do their Christmas shopping.

"Something weird is going on," Noel said to himself. When he turned back to the window, the slow-motion falling flakes and the snow already on the ground looked more unreal than ever. His heart suddenly in his throat, Noel rushed to the front door, threw it open, stepped onto the porch and ran his hand along the layer of snow on one of the shrubs. The snow wasn't cold to the touch. It wasn't even snow. It was cotton batten. Noel was able to peel away a long strip of it. He was so disconcerted by this discovery that he carefully replaced the cotton batten on the shrub.

Noel looked around to see if any of his neighbours were inspecting the fake snow. But apart from him, not a creature was stirring. He took a few tentative steps toward the street, bent down and retrieved some fresh snow from his walkway. He had sampled enough of it in his youth to recognize instant mashed potato flakes when he tasted them. His entire neighbourhood — the two or three blocks that were visible to him, at any rate — was having a freak Christmas Eve instant mashed potato snowfall. The entire block was bathed in the soft, flickering light of Christmas tree candles through frosted living room windows. From where he stood, Noel's neighbourhood was a three-dimensional Norman Rockwell Christmas tableau. "I've got to warn Beth," he said out loud.

By the time Noel had closed and bolted the door, Beth was coming down the hall with a hot toddy in each hand. "What were you up to out there?" she asked him mock-suspiciously. "You promised there would be no surprise gifts this Christmas."

Noel took the drink from Beth but his hand was trembling so violently that he had to set the glass down on the coffee table. The last thing he wanted to do was to frighten his wife. But she had to be told. "Honey," he said in a calm and deliberate voice, "have you noticed that there aren't any presents under the Christmas tree?"

Beth glanced across the room at the tree and said, "Of course not, Noel. It's still too early. Santa Claus doesn't pass until after midnight."

"After midnight," Noel said, nodding. He cleared his throat. "I guess I thought Santa operated on Greenwich Mean Time or something."

Beth took a sip of her toddy and said, "Do you suppose Emmanuel will get the chemistry set he asked for?"

Noel leaned forward to pick up his toddy, which he now desperately needed, but he stopped short of risking a sip with his unsteady hands. "Beth, there's something I —"

"Manny has been a very good boy, Noel."

"Yes he has," Noel said. "There's something I have to tell you, Beth. When I stepped outside a couple of minutes ago, I noticed the damnedest thing: The snow out there is cotton batten."

"It's beautiful, isn't it?" Beth said, gazing over Noel's shoulder at the soft, snowy light. "So dreamy and perfect."

"But it's not actual snow," Noel said.

"This is the most perfect Christmas Eve we've ever had," Beth said. A pencil-thin toddy moustache added to the frightening unfamiliarity of her face.

"And do you know what else?" Noel said, his composure melting like the flakes outside would melt if they had been made of snow,

"Everyone in the neighbourhood, including us, has candles on their Christmas tree. Surely that's a major fire hazard."

"Oh Noel, I'm so happy tonight," Beth sighed.

Perhaps it was the way she sighed his name. Perhaps it was his toddy-craving brain sending him a warning, or the lingering taste of instant mashed potato flakes in his mouth. For whatever reason, he had a fleeting suspicion at that moment that his actual name was Neil, not Noel.

Noel was relieved when Beth finally took the two empty glasses into the kitchen to finish washing up before bedtime. A couple of minutes alone would give him a chance to meditate further on what was happening to him.

"Am I losing my mind?" he asked the living room ceiling, but the ceiling offered no reply. "Have I been working too hard in recent months and now I've lost contact with reality?"

He doubted it, though the ceiling neither confirmed nor denied his fears. The fact was that he felt uncommonly lucid. So lucid that, a few moments before, when Beth had told him about her chat with Emmanuel that morning, a theory had begun to form in his mind. That morning, Emmanuel had announced that he no longer believed Santa Claus was a real person. He said Santa Claus would have to prove he was real by leaving some physical evidence of his overnight visit. That was how chemists and other scientists proved things, Manny had said. Beth told Noel how sad it made her feel that their eight year-old son was losing touch with Santa Claus. As she told him this, Noel had the inexplicable sensation that he was a character in one of those heart-warming stories books and magazines used to publish in simpler times — hopeful, uplifting stories in which a child's sense of wonder was magically restored by a special event or circumstance.

Before drawing any firm conclusions, Noel decided he would discreetly telephone a friend or family member to find out if they were having similar experiences that evening. He heard Beth softly singing "We Three Kings" in the kitchen as he tiptoed upstairs to the telephone in the den. He picked up the receiver and was about to dial when he realized that he didn't have the faintest idea who any of his family or friends were. His mind was a perfect blank. It was as though he, his wife and son and their immediate neighbourhood had been created only minutes ago by some unseen, alien intelligence.

Noel hurried downstairs and found Beth in the living room. She was placing a glass of milk and a plate of cookies on the floor by the fireplace.

"Beth," he said, "you better sit down."

His wife turned away from the fireplace, brushed a crumb from her dress and said, "Do you think Santa likes macaroons?"

"Listen to me, Beth. You and I and little Manny upstairs are characters in one of those old-fashioned Christmas stories. Whoever is writing this story didn't even bother to supply me with any friends and relatives. Our whole family is stranded inside somebody's heart-warming Yuletide yarn."

"They're low-cal macaroons," Beth said. "Besides, I don't like it when people say Santa is fat. He's not fat, he's heavy-set. There's a big difference. I put a note beside the cookies asking him to leave some kind of sign for Manny."

"Will you please listen to me, Beth? This is not real life. This is a piece of fiction. The snow outside is fake, the candles on our tree are probably fake, though I haven't checked them yet. I don't know who my parents are, and I don't even know where I work for a living."

Noel worked as a chartered accountant for the firm of Latimer, Westcott & Bedrosian. He had been with the company for nine years.

"Apparently I've been an accountant for nine years," Noel said, his voice cracking into falsetto.

"Honey, are you all right?" Beth asked him. "Maybe I put too much rum in your toddy. You look a bit flushed. I think you should get into bed, because we've got a big day tomorrow."

"You don't understand," Noel said, more harshly than he intended. "We're not real people. We're just stick-figures in some hack writer's idea of a short story. We have no free will. Everything we do depends on what our creator decides we ought to do."

"Which is why we must always be on our best behaviour, just like Manny," Beth said.

"For all we know," said Noel, tugging at his shirt collar, "there isn't even a Manny in this story. It's not like he's had any lines to speak up to now."

Just then, the sound of a sleepy voice drifted down from the top of the stairs. "Daddy?. . . Why is everybody yelling?"

Beth went to the foot of the stairs and said, "Only your father is yelling, sweetheart. But he's finished now. We're all going to bed so that Santa Claus can visit."

"Okay, but please don't fight anymore," Emmanuel said, rubbing his eyes. He staggered sleepily back down the hall to his room.

"This is a bloody conspiracy," Noel roared. "We weren't fighting. Somebody's making this up as they go along, but they don't want you or Manny to realize it. I realize it. I realize it only too well."

"Keep your voice down," Beth said. "It's almost midnight. We've got a long day tomorrow, plus Claire and Albert are coming for Christmas dinner. Let's get to bed."

Noel gazed abjectly at his wife. "Who in the hell are Claire and Albert?"

Beth glared at him. "Oh honestly, Noel. I know they're not your favourite people in the world, but she's my sister and this is no time for silly jokes. Please come to bed."

Noel now understood there was no point trying to explain their predicament to his wife. "You go up, honey," he said. "I'm sorry about the scene. I guess I'm just a bit overtired. I'll relax down here for a few minutes, then I'll join you upstairs."

"All right," said Beth. "Don't be long."

After his wife had gone, Noel grimly ensconced himself on the living room couch. If he was no more than the instrument of some two-bit writer who didn't have the common decency to sketch in a couple of parents and a friend or two for him, he wasn't going to make things easy for that writer by compliantly going off to bed. If Santa Claus was coming to the house to restore Emmanuel's faith in him, Noel wanted to be there to witness it all.

The glow of the candlelight from the Christmas tree blurred as Noel's agitation slowly turned to a sleepy calm. Stretched out on the couch, he wondered what role he was expected to play in this crudely sentimental narrative. He decided not to fight it any longer. As he drifted closer to sleep, dream-like memories of childhood Christmases with his mother and father and brothers and sisters and their dog and cat and budgie and tropical fish played faintly in Noel's mind. He had a mother and father after all, for which he was thankful — though the budgie and tropical fish struck him as unnecessary flourishes. Maybe if he went back up to the den he would be supplied with a telephone number where he could reach his folks.

Then again, it was so warm and comfortable here on the couch in the soft candlelight. . .

Sleep paid a visit, though not for long. Noel was roused by muffled sounds that seemed to be coming from inside the chimney. He sat bolt upright when he recognized human grunts along with the other sounds. He watched as black boots and red trousers fringed with white ermine descended into his fireplace. Backing out of the small cavity in the wall into the candlelit room was a heavy-set man in a Santa Claus suit and a white mohair beard.

"*Guten tag*," Santa Claus grunted as he stood up and brushed himself down.

"*Guten tag*," Noel replied, as though reading from a script.

"Are you deaf or something?" Santa Claus said. "I asked you if you got tags. I don't do tags, I just do presents."

"We've got some leftover tags from last Christmas," Noel said.

Santa Claus peered disapprovingly at the plate of cookies on the floor. "If I don't see another macaroon for the rest of eternity, it'll be too soon. Just once I wish somebody would put out a plate of blood pudding, or linguini."

Noel took a couple of steps forward and said, "You don't seem very jolly."

"I'm jolly, but I'm also businesslike," Santa Claus said. "Are you the guy with the kid who's got the doubts?"

Noel nodded.

"There's a lot of that going around," Santa Claus said. "Nowadays, people think proof is the bottom line, when it's just a second-rate version of faith."

As Santa Claus bent down to take some presents out of a canvas bag, Noel stepped closer and said, "Do you mind if I touch your beard?"

"Another doubter," Santa sighed, his arms laden with gifts. "Touch away, Noel, but keep your hands above the belt and get a move on. I don't have all night."

Noel went up to Santa Claus and gently touched his snowy beard. It wasn't made of mohair, or cotton batten. It was a beard.

"Now listen to me carefully," Santa Claus said. "Inside that big box with the pukey yellow wrapping paper is the kid's chemistry set. I put some special instructions in the box for him. If he follows my instructions, the magic potion he makes will guarantee that he believes in me forever and ever. All his doubts will instantly vanish and —. . . Jesus, even I don't believe this crap."

"What's wrong?" Noel said.

"I can't go through with this cockamamey magic potion subplot," Santa Claus said. He glared up at the ceiling and bellowed, as though to some unseen being who was directing the scene, "Why don't you get a normal day-job like everybody else instead of tormenting innocent readers with mawkish stories like this?"

"Easy now, Santa," said Noel. "Maybe you should sit down for a minute."

"I don't have time to sit down. I'm Santa Claus. It's people like you who've got it made."

"How do you mean?" Noel said.

"Reality is overrated, Noel. The life you've got in this story has its advantages, even if it's drab by any literary standard. Think about it: If this was real life, you'd be expected to report back to work at Latimer, Westcott & Bedrosian in a couple of days. Nobody who's reading this expects you to do any actual work for that firm, now or ever."

"You mean because I'm not real?" Noel asked.

"Because you're more real than real. Because you're well taken care of. You could just as easily have wound up dying of consumption in a nineteenth century novel, or trapped in one of those cyberpunk CD-ROMs science-fiction writers are cranking out these days. Instead you're stuck in this relatively nice house, talking to relatively jolly old St. Nick. You should count your blessings."

Noel reflected on that for a moment. Then he looked at Santa Claus and said, "What about Manny? If there's no magic potion in the chemistry set, how is he supposed to believe in you again?"

"Don't you get it?" Santa Claus said. "That's your job. That's the hackneyed theme of this whole story. It's a story of faith and acceptance – the kind of smarmy tale I'm forever being parachuted into, as if I don't have enough to do. I thought I was supposed to give the kid the potion recipe, but you had even worse doubts than Emmanuel, which is why you're down here talking to me when you should be upstairs in bed with that cute wife of yours. My advice to you is to be thankful that you've got a wife, a kid and a couple of city blocks to move around in."

"But what will happen to us when this story comes to an end?" Noel asked Santa Claus.

"That's something to ask your clergyman," Santa Claus said. "I've got to fly. I put some stuff under the tree for you and Beth, too." He hoisted his bag over his shoulder. "What are you waiting for? Give me a leg-up."

Noel helped Santa Claus back into the fireplace. Santa's last words to him from the top of the chimney were: "You've got a creosote situation here, my friend." Then the house was still and silent again.

On his way to bed, Noel looked in on Emmanuel. He sat gently on the edge of the bed and touched his son's shoulder. The boy awoke. Noel said to him: "There really is a Santa Claus, Manny. I just had a very interesting chat with him."

Emmanuel yawned and said, "When do I get to make the magic potion that makes me believe in him forever and ever?"

"You don't get to make it," Noel said tenderly. "The magic potion was dropped from the story at the last minute. You just have to bring yourself to believe in him. I can help, son, because I believe in him now. I believe in a whole lot of things."

"Right-o, Dad," Emmanuel said and closed his eyes.

Then Noel found his own bed and let himself drift into the peaceful cottony night next to Beth's warm body. Soon a serene faith in the wisdom and good will of his creator enveloped him.

Beth stirred and said, "Is it morning yet?"

"Not for a long time," Noel answered contentedly. As Beth's breathing deepened, he gazed with child-like wonder through an opening in the curtains at the softly falling flakes of instant mashed potatoes.

THE END OF THE YEAR

As the calendar year draws to a close, the pressure to mark its passage with unbridled merriment reaches an apex. Gala balls, dinner-dances and lavish house parties are organized to help us ring out the old year in high spirits. If we haven't been invited to any of these functions, there's always the cheery prospect of watching the ageless Dick Clark usher in the new year on television. But regardless of how we wind up spending the evening, it climaxes the same everywhere at the stroke of midnight with the chanting of an incoherent song called "Auld Lang Syne".

To be perfectly honest, I find the lyrics of "Auld Lang Syne" too esoteric to inspire sentiments of any kind, let alone dewy-eyed nostalgia. What in heaven's name do the words auld lang syne mean? Are they Sanskrit? Esperanto? Why haven't more people questioned the implications of what they're expressing in this song before locking arms to belt it out at midnight? How do they know "Auld Land Syne" isn't a neo-fascist call for Scottish domination of the world?

Before you conclude I'm not much fun to be around on New Year's Eve, I should point out that I've been known to sing The Indecipherable New Year's Song like everyone else — though I draw the line at blowing a noisemaker in people's faces. But I've always felt somewhat ambivalent about New Year's Eve festivities. Sometimes I think I would prefer it if the old year would shuffle quietly away while I'm not looking, rather than stand on a metaphorical pier and wave a metaphorical hankie at me as I sail off into the future. And yet a part of me longs for the sense of completion and closure a New Year's Eve bash can bring to the passing year.

A genuine spirit of bacchanalia is almost as hard to find as it is to spell in these prim and self-conscious times. All of us secretly long to let what's left of our hair down at least one night of the year. For this reason, New Year's Eve festivities have a kind of tidal effect on the blood. The approach of the first hour of the dawning year, especially when compounded by intoxicants, seems to lend the words auld lang syne emotional weight, if not outright meaning.

For several years when I was young, I operated under the mistaken impression that The Indecipherable New Year's Song was called "For Old Anxiety". I even formed a theory of why the song was called that. The way I saw it, "For Old Anxiety" was a song about exorcising the fears and worries of the outgoing year through the traditional escapist strategy of "raising a cup of kindness", which is a Scottish euphemism for having a wee snort, which is a further Scottish euphemism for consuming an alcoholic beverage.

Even as a youngster, I was able to decipher the opening lines of Robert Burns' little ode. They were: "Should auld acquaintance be forgot and never brought to mind?" The word *auld* was the way people spelled the word *old* in olden times. That much I knew. But the line as a whole struck me as the sentiment of someone who was considering the idea of making a clean break from the past, rather than trying to remember it. I interpreted the line as the deliberations of someone who was thinking of erasing all memories of "auld acquaintance" who may have caused offence, injury or anxiety. In the third and fourth line of the song, the person pondering this break from the people who once were near and dear to her expresses the sheer magnitude of her problem: Not only must she forget "auld acquaintance", she must forget the past itself — the "days of auld anxiety".

Apparently I got the song wrong.

Having spent countless hours poring over the sub-atomic typeface of my Compact Edition of the Oxford English Dictionary, I am now in a position to decode "Auld Lang Syne" in its entirety.

Syne is a word of "obscure philological significance" common to Scottish and northern English dialects and possibly derived from Old Norse. It means "before now" or "ago". *Syne* can also mean "at a later time" or "afterwards", which shows one of the linguistic drawbacks of Old Norse. But Burns undoubtedly intended the word to signify the past.

Lang is Old English for "long" and corresponds to the Scottish *launge*, which is merely a long Scottish way of spelling and pronouncing "long". Burns probably threw the redundant word *auld* in front of *lang syne* because, like so many people from the British Isles, he was excessively fond of the word *auld*.

Burns' famous New Year's song is a paean to nostalgia, a fond toast to all the blessings of the past and a fitting way to bring this book to a close. In the interest of clarity and behavioural correctness, I have translated the song into contemporary English. Feel free to sing this version when the clock strikes midnight next New Year's Eve, whether you're a face in a crowd or home alone.

> *If we've lost track of friends we knew*
> *And our memory is a haze,*
> *If we've lost track of friends we knew*
> *And all the good old days,*
> *For all the good old days, my friend,*
> *For all the good old days,*
> *We'll raise a glass of Diet Coke*
> *For all the good old days.*